Library Girls of New York

A Secret Place

Carolyn Rhodes

Carolyn Rhodes

Library Girls of New York

A Secret Place

Carolyn Rhodes

ISBN 978-1-7339165-5-4
Library of Congress Control Number: 2019916362

BORGO
PUBLISHING

www.borgopublishing.com

Text and cover design: Borgo Publishing, Tuscaloosa, Alabama
Cover image: McGraw Rotunda, NYPL Main Library.

Printed in the USA

Surplus wealth is a sacred trust which its possessor is bound to administer in his lifetime for the good of the community.

—ANDREW CARNEGIE

Mom, Irene, Dad holding me, and Helen in front of Tompkins Square Library

I would like to thank
Theresa and Joseph, my parents

Helen and Irene, my sisters

Casey Julian, my son, for his tech help

New York Public Library Digital Collection

AND

The librarians and philanthropists
of the New York Public Library
who have given us so much
to be thankful for.

Table of Contents

Preface | **vii**

Chapter One | **1**
Home Sweet Library

Chapter Two | **6**
Greatest Generation Parents

Chapter Three | **17**
Tompkins Square Historic District

Chapter Four | **42**
School Days, P.S. 122, Lower East Side

Chapter Five | **53**
St. George, Staten Island
New York City

Chapter Six | **76**
Turning Point, 1966–1971

Chapter Seven | **88**
Curtain Call, 1971–1976

PREFACE

Andrew Carnegie Libraries

FROM APPROXIMATELY 1910 TO the 1970s, the New York Public Library (NYPL) offered free apartments to include salary for its custodian families. The hours were on call seven days a week for the many duties required to fulfill the 24/7 commitment. Jacks-of-all-trades would answer the call. Joseph Mitchell, my dad, was one of them.

I can account only for Dad and his four library girls, Theresa (Mom), Helen, Irene, and me. Our residences were under the umbrella of Andrew Carnegie Libraries.

The Carnegie family immigrated to the United States from Scotland. Between 1883 and 1929, there were 2,509 Carnegie libraries funded throughout the world. The very first library funded was built in Andrew Carnegie's birth place, Dunfermline, Fife, Scotland.

In the early years, there were 65 Carnegie libraries throughout New York City. Now there are 53 remaining according to the Historic District Council of New York survey in 2009. There were approximately 30 live-in libraries scattered throughout the five boroughs of New York City. Today these apartments are empty.

The last NYPL family occupant retired in 2005. Thanks to Andrew Carnegie's generous gift of over five million dollars early twentieth century. This memoir covers around 35 years of my family living inside three of the NYPL apartment branches.

My dad got his first live-in library job in 1938 at the Rivington Street Branch in lower Manhattan. Erected in 1905, the Rivington Street Branch, a Beaux-Art structure, was the first Carnegie Library to have an outside roof reading area. Dad was later transferred to the Tompkins Square Branch Library, also a Beaux-Art building and classically

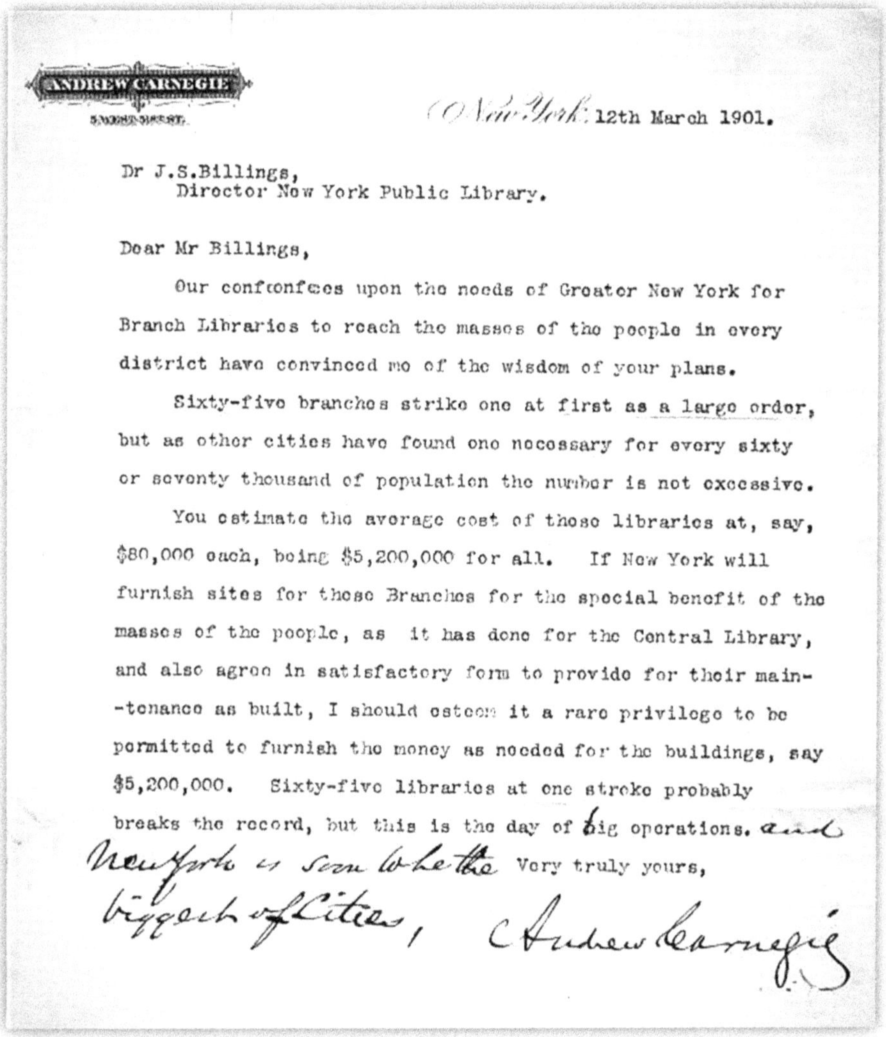

ANDREW CARNEGIE

New York, 12th March 1901.

Dr J.S.Billings,
Director New York Public Library.

Dear Mr Billings,

Our conferences upon the needs of Greater New York for Branch Libraries to reach the masses of the people in every district have convinced me of the wisdom of your plans.

Sixty-five branches strike one at first as a large order, but as other cities have found one necessary for every sixty or seventy thousand of population the number is not excessive.

You estimate the average cost of these libraries at, say, $80,000 each, being $5,200,000 for all. If New York will furnish sites for these Branches for the special benefit of the masses of the people, as it has done for the Central Library, and also agree in satisfactory form to provide for their main-tenance as built, I should esteem it a rare privilege to be permitted to furnish the money as needed for the buildings, say $5,200,000. Sixty-five libraries at one stroke probably breaks the record, but this is the day of big operations. and New York is soon to be the biggest of Cities,

Very truly yours,

Andrew Carnegie

Andrew Carnegie, letter to Dr. Billings, NYPL, 1901, courtesy of NYPL Digital Library

styled in Italian Renaissance Revival. Our final library apartment was the St. George Library Branch in Staten Island, New York. It was a brick building sitting high on a hill, built in 1905. This library was a train and a ferry boat ride away from our Tompkins Square apartment on East 10th Street, Manhattan. Andrew Carnegie's gift to the New York Public Library (NYPL) served Dad and his library girls well and for that I am appreciative.

CHAPTER ONE

Home Sweet Library Home

An unexamined life is not worth living

—SOCRATES

ONCE UPON A TIME, in real time, there were three sisters, Helen, Irene, and Carolyn Mitchell, who lived with their parents in an iconic place, the New York Public Library. Many remarked they thought living in a public library meant one loved reading and that it would be easy to check out a library book if you lived there. While that is true, it was home, literally, our home sweet home.

Telling others that we lived all those years of growing up in a library was often met with one eyebrow raised or wide eyes bulging from their sockets.

Most new friends, would ask, "You live where?"

Our peers thought it was unbelievable. While people lived in apartments or private brownstones in the city, our library dwelling at the Tompkins Square Branch was located on third floor of the building. Some classmates heard I lived in the library and their curiosity got the best of them in elementary school. The usual question, "You live in the liberry . . . on a bookshelf?!"

It was the perfect tease coming from the mouths of babes until a few boys followed me home and met my dad. He was called upon to take care of the troublemakers, especially noisy ones or anyone bullying his girls.

New York Public Library Stephen A. Schwarzman Building

My second library home, the St. George Branch on Staten Island, was different. We had a separate private entrance on the Central Avenue side. It was a relief after parading past the main desk at Tompkins Square Branch every day where we waited for a friendly wave and then a nod to get up the staircase to our apartment on the third floor.

We lived in a private apartment in a public institution. Sometimes we referred to it as "our secret place."

Sadly, the main characters of this book, Theresa and Joseph Mitchell, my mom and dad, passed away many years after their retirement to Toms River, New Jersey.

Once my sisters, Helen and Irene, agreed to share our story, the pieces came together. I realized it was more than just our story, but, rather a unique story of a lifestyle only a handful of families have lived.

The many philanthropists, volunteers, and those unforgettable librarians deserve much applause as there would be no story about the Library Girls of New York without these people woven into our history. The branch librarians who warmly referred to us as, the Library Girls or Mr. and Mrs. Mitchell's girls remain in our fondest memories. It is who we were, who we are.

I've gathered up the proof that we are the last of an era of family occupants who resided in a library branch in the New York City area. It is a time that will never be recorded again in history as we knew it.

To write this book, I used keepsake albums and yearbooks, where, stuffed in between pages were scented pressed flowers and faded paper notes, all remained well preserved. There were boxes of loose photos, borders of white scallop-edging well-worn out from the sands of time. Aging alongside the creases, wrinkles, and faded Kodachrome photos, I see three little library girls surrounded by loving people.

I could hear Mom say, "Smile for the birdie, don't move." Our shadows had to be directly behind us and the sun in front for the best results.

The memorabilia are vivid on visualization. Poetic scribblings, handwritten on separate pieces of paper, Helen's book of flowers and needlework, and Irene's first poetry book. Each of us kept a set of Mom's hand-sewn curtains.

Mom and I embroidered swans and ducks onto hand towels. We made pretty aprons, no two alike. She took us to the local Woolworth's Five and Dime store. There we purchased our supply of the finest boxed handkerchiefs and ribbons of all sizes and colors to make special handmade aprons for our relatives and the librarians we were close to. These were the perfect holiday gift.

A librarian at the Oak files, referencing, courtesy of NYPL Digital Library

Staff librarians watched over us as we grew up at Tompkins Square Library. Years passed before I opened the grammar school graduation albums. The pages included endearing notes of best wishes from our branch librarians. I recall that when we moved to the St. George Branch on Staten Island, Mom exchanged holiday cards with them. Sometimes a call came in from a librarian to see how the family was doing.

Having librarians around was a perk. If we needed information or a book from another branch, they never hesitated to go past their main duties to get what any of us needed.

We were an NYPL family and joined in all the holiday parties. Getting dressed up for the Christmas parties, going to the main library, we walked through the most impressive marble interior, sculptures, and art surrounding us. City socialites, many donors, enjoyed the festivities. All the staff members from the New York City branches were invited. Mom wore her handmade chiffon maroon dress with gloves and hat or her one-of-a-kind taffeta dress. We little library girls wore ribbons and bows.

Custodians of the NYPL became experts in heating these large buildings. The coals burned down to hot ash until sunrise, at which time, new coals had to be added. Dad was up long before any of us to prepare for the day ahead. On snow days, he shoveled snow and deiced the steps and sidewalks as soon as the snow fell or ice began to form.

By the time the first librarians entered and removed their winter hats and coats on cold mornings, they began the day in comfort. Patrons entered a clean, quiet place to read or learn. A penny tumbling down onto Dad's shiny waxed and buffed floor was the loudest sound amid the silence. For some, it was a jolt and a body stretch before returning to reading or writing.

The quiet endures, the free-of-charge still exists, and the calm remains. But the differences are evident. Library cards are plastic, and the file card catalogue oak cabinets are no longer needed as the libraries have kept pace with modern times. Times have changed, but the voices we took for granted still resonate clearly as we cling to them with reverence.

McGraw Rotunda, NYPL Main Library, courtesy of Steven Brooke

A good love story stands the test of time. In my next chapter, Theresa Milo and Joseph Mitchell, Mom and Dad, have their own "how they met" story. I state unequivocally that the Library Girls of New York were fortunate to be the children of Greatest Generation parents. It all began when Theresa met Joseph at the workplace. The story, like any good love story from almost a century ago, has its place in family love stories. We never forgot their memories. And, over the years we grew up we heard their stories many times.

CHAPTER TWO

Greatest Generation Parents

Sometimes you will never know the value of a moment until it becomes a memory.

—DR. SEUSS

A Courtship

Theresa Milo, the oldest of nine children, was born in New York City in August 1913, to Angelina DeVito Milo and Stephen Milo. Stephen owned a horse-drawn carriage and delivered ice to families on the lower east side of Manhattan. Refrigerators were not in most homes until the 1930s. My grandfather made a good living during lean times when families had only ice boxes.

Theresa Milo

When Theresa was a teenager, she took over the housekeeping and cooking to care for her younger siblings when her mother, Angelina, became ill. Despite all she had to do,

Theresa completed dressmaking school. After graduation, she got a job at Bergdorf Goodman Department Store (BG) on Fifth Avenue in New York City. It was where she met the love of her life, Joseph Mitchell, circa 1933.

Theresa and Joseph Mitchell on their wedding day

Romance was in the air at BG and within the heartbeat of America when Theresa met Joseph, around 1933, the post–Great Depression years. The market was slow to recover but Theresa got work a short time after Joseph was employed at BG.

Joseph Mitchell, a handsome man of Polish heritage with light brown hair, aqua eyes, a well-sculpted nose, and fair skin, was born in Chicago in 1911. Around 1929 as the Depression hit, Joseph hitched a ride to Florida and then to New York City for the prospect of finding a good job. When Bergdorf Goodman hired him, his New York City life began and he never looked back to Chicago.

Fashion in New York City has kept up with trends regardless of the economy and that meant that fashion thrived throughout the world even during the Great Depression. When Bergdorf Goodman opened a new store at 58th and Fifth Avenue, Joseph was hired to run the elevators. Theresa Milo, his destiny, would eventually be hired as a dressmaker.

The workplace rules were in place and employees did not question them. Mom said, "Once you punched the clock, it was time to work and you didn't dare come in late. You got docked or fired."

She would tell us about her supervisor, "Clients came in to be fitted, but I was too shy to talk so I let my supervisor do all the talking while I pinned the hems and took measurements. My specialty was draping. I was an apparel designer, but I got paid as a dressmaker. We worked with fine silks, velvet and satin. The sewing had to be perfect." I remember now that Mom made her sisters' wedding gowns.

2011 Bergdorf Goodman corner, courtesy of Bing/Skyscraper.com

Mom described the sewing machines and how they sounded in unison in a factory setting; how the pedals beneath the machine gently squealed on rotation as her foot gently hit the pedal. The faint sound of threading through the eye of a needle, and how the rhythm of slow to faster to very fast and then a full stop. The patterned fabric had to be manually reset in between two guides, one on each side of the needle.

Mom remembered very clearly, "You didn't dare look up when we were at the sewing machines. I was lucky because I got to work at the pattern table too and the draping for a custom fitting." She clarified, "Buttons and trimmings added a classy look to the fabrics. My supervisor asked me for suggestions in the very final creation of an outfit, but she got the credit."

There were two private elevators that ran between the seventh and ninth floors. These went to the penthouse suite, which was the Goodman family residence. Dad worked the elevators to transport shoppers and employees.

While his job seemed simple, transporting employees up and down the elevator shaft, maintaining good communications was just as important. He was the first person to greet the employees and carry on cordial conversations about weather, traffic and, sports.

The elevators were as ornate as the interior floors, decorated in floral wallpapers, matching in elegance to the trending Art Deco skyscrapers going up in the 1930s, like the Empire State and the Chrysler Building. Bergdorf Goodman was built in the Beaux-Art style.

Architects were mindful of exquisite details creating the eye candy of the day in New York City, inside and outside. Dad, who had an eye for beautiful architecture, reminisced about the Bergdorf Goodman architecture and his appreciation for art and the engineers who laid out the blueprints for the city's skyline: "Bergdorf Goodman Department Store was a work of art in elegance, from ceilings to Italian marble floors. There's a lot of talented people who know engineering and design. They made the city skyline."

Elevator operators needed to be strong and have a pleasant disposition. Dad shared his baseball knowledge and kept scores for employees who waited for his elevator. Morning and evening, there was a lot of talk about sports and who the best players were of just about any sport.

Dad liked working and getting the day started happy. He often mentioned how baseball changed the day, "We forgot our hardships and I always had the latest scores, the news on the Babe [Babe Ruth], Lou Gehrig and Joe DiMaggio." Dad enjoyed the camaraderie, "Some of the guys were players in their spare time and some were even in amateur leagues, like me. It was a nice break from reality. I wanted to impress your mother whenever she was on an elevator too, so she thought maybe I was a smart man."

Every morning, afternoon, and evening, fashionably dressed ladies, like Mom, piled into Dad's elevator. The Goodman's love stories were the most popular gossip. Herman started the company in 1899 and his son Edwin kept up the store. But when Edwin's son Andrew Goodman grew up and took over, his vision took the world by surprise.

He surpassed his dad's elegance and charm. He traveled the world in search of new fabrics and learned many languages. Society pages kept Bergdorf Goodman in their radar. There was always news on Andrew, and the elevator gossip covered all the latest Goodman's penthouse suite parties, art exhibits at Bergdorf Goodman, and the celebrities in their social circle who visited the penthouse.

Office gossip started in the elevator. Rumors were passed around like a winter cold. Andrew Goodman and Dita, despite the gossip, did not break up, as some ladies hoped. It was unusual in the 1930s for men to marry women like Dita, who was divorced, from Cuba, and had a child from another marriage. But Dita was one of a kind, like Andrew. She was also independent. They made a power couple.

Mom said, "No one believed it would ever last, and some of the girls who worked with Mr. Goodman had crushes on him, even flirting with him after he was married. He was handsome and a charmer. I only liked Joseph. I was too shy to look another man in the eye."

Joseph's perspective of it was that "those ladies liked gossip. A few ladies would squeeze into the elevator, right next to Andrew. He was a gentleman. He was pleasant and never made a fuss when they got a little too close. What man would mind the attention of those beautiful models and pretty office gals?" Dad continued, "Look, the man was well educated, spoke several languages and traveled the world. Dita was a smart cookie too and sophisticated. She had her own business as an art curator, showed off a lot of new artists' works. They were a match made in heaven, like me and Theresa."

Dating the elevator guy had its perks. When the clock struck noon, sewing machines turned off, with the punch out timecards in hand, purses and sweaters on the other, dressmakers followed Theresa's cue when her knight in shining armor arrived to deliver "his girls" to the cafeteria. Empty stomachs churned; bodies jumped when the elevator came to a dead stop. Hardly noticing the jolting and the speed, the dressmaker girls got to be the first on the cafeteria line, thanks to Theresa's boyfriend, Joseph.

On the way down, after lunch, Joseph showed up on time, packing them in like a can of sardines. Joseph gave the cue, "Going down."

The ladies huddled together and giggled about how their ears popped. Fullness gave way to a few thumps, bounces, and a bump or two as Joseph lined his elevator up with the marble-floor hallway. Joseph looked forward as he spoke to his passengers as he manually locked the metal accordion gate in tight.

"Watch your step ladies. Have a wonderful afternoon," he winked.

Joseph was looking forward to the evening when he and Theresa could take a stroll through Central Park in the light of spring and hot summer city nights.

Baseball was the one sport almost every American loved. It had staying power through the highs and lows of the times, any economy. Joseph loved the sport. It was his joy for an entire lifetime.

Play Ball

Dad played many sports over the years, but baseball was his game. He played during the 1930s on local teams at Ebbets Field in Brooklyn. Local teams used the field when the Dodgers were playing away games or when World Series played there. Dad took Mom on their first date to a ballgame that he played in.

During the Depression and its recovery, everyone knew of the Brooklyn Dodgers. Diehard bandstand fans were as vital as the team. They brought in the crowds. Famous ballplayers, Joe DiMaggio, Lou Gehrig and Babe Ruth, took pay cuts during the Depression years when America needed a friend. Legends stepped up to the plate.

World Series were won and lost on that almost sacred land now covered over by housing apartments. But its hero ballplayers remain in baseball's memory. Dad once told me, "If it wasn't for baseball, I don't think I would have survived all the hardships."

Joseph (right) at Ebbets Field, 1937

Jackie Robinson, courtesy of NYPL Digital Collection

Ebbets Field was as famous as the sport of baseball itself. Although today it is no longer a field, the memories live on as the home of the Dodgers from 1913 to 1957.

Casey Stengel hit his first home run in 1913 and Jackie Robinson became the first African American rookie for the Dodgers making his first historic home run at Ebbets. The last echoes of great moments in baseball resonate to this day as we remember these legends of baseball. Dad said that Robinson would be one of the greats, and he is. He said, "It's about time. Who cares what color you are! Robinson has gone down in history. Play Ball #42!"

Fast forward to the days when we lived at the St. George Library Branch on Staten Island. Dad made sure to reserve the TV, our only black and white, for World Series games. It was Dad's time to get a couple of pals over. The living room transformed into a man cave.

The smell of Dad's corn pipe smoke billowed out of his big ashtray, almost forgotten until the "boys" all got together and lit up their cigarettes, pipes, and occasional cigars. That's what a Saturday afternoon smelled like during the World Series with escalating chants coming from that room, "Come on you bums, get on base," or "Referee called it, foul ball," or, "Two strikes , one more strike, you're out!"

A raucous was heard, as if they were at Yankee Stadium especially when or if a grand slam or a home run happened. Every fan waited for it. Those were the days of Joe DiMaggio, Mickey Mantle, Roger Maris, Willie Mays, and Jackie Robinson.

Dad would tell us and his fellow baseball cronies, "I could run like a rabbit, but guys like Babe Ruth were 6 Foot four. I never made major league, too short. Besides I have a family to feed first. When I was young, they didn't pay much."

Our dad finally told us that he was born in Chicago and had left behind his brothers and sisters, and his father. He often told us about the days when hard times hit, when the stock market crashed in 1929. He spoke about the long lines in the cold weather. He lamented, "Many times, I had to choose between a cigarette and a bowl of soup. Money and food were scarce. Families went hungry. Everyone was looking for work. There was no welfare or even social security. Americans were on their own with no financial handouts." His stories never changed especially about my two grandmothers. He often reminisced his loss. These were the rare times when a man could get teary eyed and share his grief.

Dad told his story from time to time, "My father was strict after my mother died."

When we library girls were grown up, he visited with his lost relatives in Arizona and Chicago and further explained, "You get to understand as a grown-up life wasn't easy. My father worked long days to put food on the table for all four of his children. We had to take care of ourselves, get up for school and wash our own cloths. I thought I should run away from home. I would be less of a burden, one less mouth to feed. It was good to see my sister and brothers again and their children."

After a time working at Bergdorf Goodman, Dad got his first job cleaning the marble statues at the Main Library on Fifth Avenue and 42nd Street. Within a year, he was hired as a custodian. He moved up in rank from the main branch as a maintenance man to custodian of the Rivington Street Branch. It was his first live-in apartment, located in lower Manhattan. At the time, Mom and Dad were newly married.

Custodian positions required someone who was able to move about and had wide-ranging skills beyond cleaning, waxing floors, opening and closing library doors, keeping patrons quiet and being present when needed. He made himself indispensable.

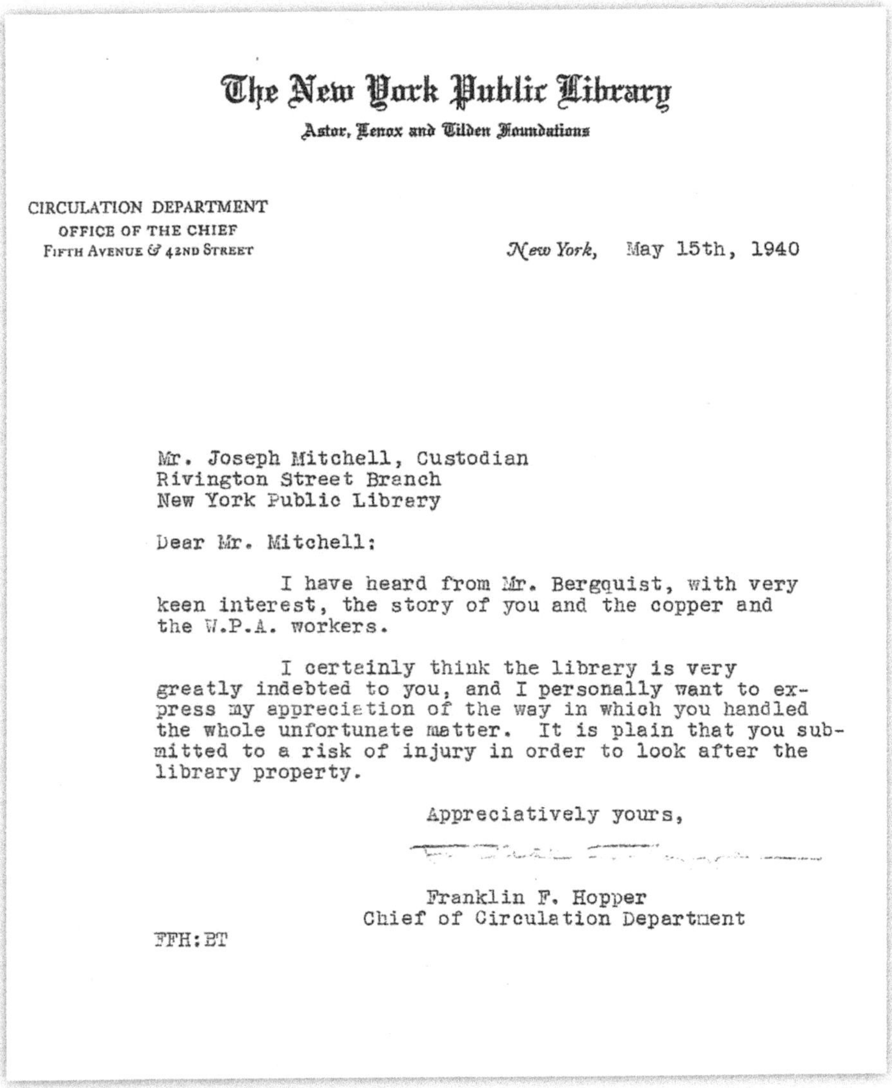

The New York Public Library

Astor, Lenox and Tilden Foundations

CIRCULATION DEPARTMENT
OFFICE OF THE CHIEF
FIFTH AVENUE & 42ND STREET

New York, May 15th, 1940

Mr. Joseph Mitchell, Custodian
Rivington Street Branch
New York Public Library

Dear Mr. Mitchell:

I have heard from Mr. Bergquist, with very keen interest, the story of you and the copper and the W.P.A. workers.

I certainly think the library is very greatly indebted to you, and I personally want to express my appreciation of the way in which you handled the whole unfortunate matter. It is plain that you submitted to a risk of injury in order to look after the library property.

Appreciatively yours,

Franklin F. Hopper
Chief of Circulation Department

FFH:BT

Letter from Franklin Hopper to Joseph Mitchell, 1940, courtesy of NYPL Digital Library

The New York Public Library

Astor, Lenox and Tilden Foundations

OFFICE OF THE DIRECTOR
5TH AVENUE & 42ND STREET

New York, May 15, 1940

Mr. Joseph Mitchell
Rivington Street Branch
New York Public Library
61 Rivington Street
New York City

Dear Mr. Mitchell:

Let me send you this word of thanks and commendation for what you did in connection with the safeguarding of Library and City property last Thursday, the 9th. Mr. Bergquist reported how alert you were and how bravely you defended not only yourself but City property when the W.P.A. workmen were trying to steal it. On behalf of the Library I want to thank you and assure you of our appreciation.

Truly yours,

H. M. Lydenberg,
Director

DS

Letter from H.M. Lydenberg to Joseph Mitchell, 1940, courtesy of NYPL Digital Library

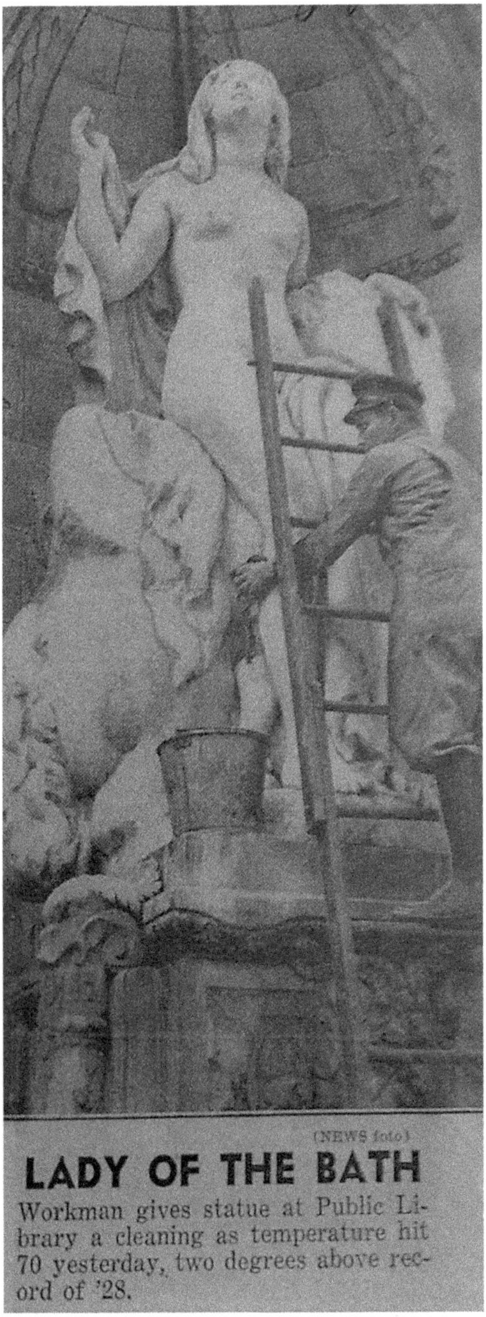

Joseph Mitchell cleaning Lady of the Bath statue at NYPL Main Library

In May 1939, when Dad was a newly hired custodian at Rivington Street Branch in downtown Manhattan, criminal activity was reported. An alert letter from the main branch warned that acquisitions of copper were being stolen throughout the city branches. Dad protected the library's precious copper artifacts as best he could by keeping an eye open for suspicious activity.

His instincts kicked in when temporary workers, hired through Roosevelt's New Deal Program, showed up. One day he caught them red-handed with a few copper artifacts hidden under their coats. He kept the men from leaving the library and locked them in until the New York Police Department showed up.

Following his heroic actions, Police Commissioner Louis Valentine and Mayor LaGuardia honored him with a new title, building control director of the Rivington Street Branch.

CHAPTER THREE

Tompkins Square Historic District

I don't know where I'm going, but I'm on my way.
—CARL SANDBURG

Tompkins Square Library

The Tompkins Square Library was built in 1904 in the Beaux-Art style and was classically styled Italian Renaissance Revival. Our apartment was on the top floor overlooking the East 11th Street back alley.

When Dad took the new job at the Tompkins Square Branch in 1941, the head librarian knew that Dad caught the copper thieves at Rivington Street Branch, but in no way was he going live off his laurels. He continued to learn on the job and became indispensable among his lady librarians. Can you imagine all the things that could break down or simply go wrong in one day?

In addition to repairs and stoking the coals, Dad knew about plumbing, electrical work, and carpentry. He read all the how-to books. If a windowsill was warped and needed to be planed, he would take it to his basement workshop where he had all the tools he needed. Irene found Dad's workshop fascinating, "I made it my duty to watch the precise back-and-forth of the handsaw. I considered the ensuing mounds of sawdust amazing enough, but the way Dad flexed the mus-

Joseph in front of the Tompkins Square Library Branch, 1944

cles in his arms as he worked proved he was as powerful as Samson in the movie, Samson and Delilah." In1951, I had my best Christmas. Everything, all the secrecy, made sense that very morning. Dad said we couldn't follow him downstairs anymore to his workshop and gave an excuse that it was dangerous, especially with power tools. After our gifts were opened, I knew Santa's elves had been busy helping Dad in the library workshop making a crib for my beautiful rag doll that Mom had made. The crib even had wheels. My three-foot tall rag doll had embroidered lips, eyes and lashes and wore a chiffon maroon silk dress and had a hat and ballet slippers to match.

When Uncle Tom, Mom's brother, returned from World War II he brought us three dolls from Hungary. I got the biggest because Uncle Tom was my godfather. Mom said these dolls were to be cherished. They were in Hungarian dress with ribbons flowing freely and had hand-painted faces and delicately hand-sewn bodies. The three Hungarian dolls took up residency alongside my rag doll and ballerina doll in their new home, the crib that Dad constructed.

Dad used his carpentry skills around the library too. Besides planing the windowsills, he fixed shelves, built some new ones, and made frames for several lithographs of famous painters from around the world. Framed art was strategically placed on the library walls, above the bookshelves. Paintings, sculptures, and special collections were enclosed within glass cases for viewing only.

The main entrance of the library was located on East 10th Street. The building stood out as a centerpiece of architecture between Avenues A and B. The brownstones nearest to the corner of Avenue A were single family homes and a few doctors' offices. Tenements closest to the library and the Avenue B corner were colorful. We had a barber shop and a candy store at that corner.

Our spacious apartment had plenty of light and privacy with a very large kitchen. The hallway off from the kitchen led to a living room with a door to another passageway; and from that corridor to two connected bedrooms—one directly across from the living room, the other on the far side of the hallway, across from the front door. Three of the rooms looked out onto the East 11th Street alleyway where clotheslines crossed over and under. These were drilled into brick walls outside each apartment back alley window of the railroad flats.

Our apartment, on the top floor of the library at Tompkins Square, was roomy. Our kitchen was always bright even when it was a dull weather day. Mom had her dish and glass collections nicely displayed in cabinets surrounding one wall although it was getting crowded. These rainbow-colored collections were bought at the local Woolworth's five and dime store, usually for a special occasion, like Mother's Day or a birthday. They cost anywhere from a quarter to a dollar. Woolworth's five and dime had carnival glass in many shapes, sizes, and color patterns.

Me, Mom and Irene on Tompkins Square Park sidewalk across from the library.

Also, on display in our wall-to-wall cabinets were the rose-gold trimmed dishes and the latest edition of the apple design complete set. Every piece setting was free with groceries. We had to fill several stamp books in order to obtain one free dish or bowl a week.

On the back wall was a dumbwaiter with a calendar on it. The dumbwaiter was used for heavy items that could not be hauled by walking up three flights of stairs. Most significant was when Dad sent up ice cream sodas, which he made downstairs in the staff lunchroom kitchen every Sunday. Once the dumbwaiter headed up, we were summoned by Dad yelling up, "Come and get it." We loved root beer soda and plenty of ice cream, topped with whipped cream and a cherry. The pink table came along with us throughout the years, every move, every house. Mom did some reupholstering of the seat cushions and Dad painted the wrought iron trimmings design of leaves and flowers. I think it was treated like a family heirloom. A leaf was available if we had company. We often had Mom's family, our aunts and uncles, over. That's when they all lived on the lower east side, close to our library, before they moved to Queens.

Me eating cake with Helen and Irene to the right.

There was only one clothesline hooked from the library apartment to the other side of the brick tenement across from us. Mom called it Busy Body Alley especially in the summer. Housewives and children sat on the fire escape, precariously dangling barefoot, fishing for a breeze. Window fans didn't give much comfort on a humid day and no one had air-conditioning. Weather was a main topic and came along with the neighborhood gossip, which spread easily from person to person.

Imagine doing laundry without a washing machine, hanging each sheet, shirt, and blouse, and yes, underwear out to dry. Mom did it at least twice a week, weather permitting. Steel pulleys were drilled into the outside brick wall and that was our dryer of the day—a clothesline bearing underwear of all sizes, a private preview of information. We girls thought the show quite funny while at the same time neighbors politely waved across the alley to each other and commented about the heat. A little spying never went unnoticed by Mom. One could tell a lot about someone from their hanging out to dry garments, all sizes. The large lady's corset, and some worn out sheets hung shamelessly as the sunlight reveal pointed to the proud immigrants who arrived via Ellis Island.

When a big story hit the news, back-alley voices conversed from across their back windows, often about neighborhood crime. One story got the attention of many and like a wildfire, it spread that fast. A child was hit by a car on Avenue A. The news traveled from the front-page news to the two housewives chatting back and forth while grabbing wooden clothes pins from a heavy bag hanging outside the window. The news was then ready to travel like a virus to the next neighbor and finally to the ladies on the stoop, who very rapidly got the attention of anyone who walked by, stopped for a polite hello and then walked away with an earful. The acoustics from a back alley was good enough for anyone to get the news before the next newspaper article came out. There were real stories which occurred around the city.

A housewife spoke with authority, "It was on the front page, right around the corner from here. It was a cryin' shame what happened to that kid. The driver hit him and kept on going. They caught the S.O.B.," she screamed out in frustration and anger. Mom sometimes joined in politely, "It is a darn shame. You never know what could happen. I hold my children's hands when we cross the street. These cars fly around the corners. You can't look away for one second."

The squeaking of the pully, the perched birds singing, and kids playing stick ball was a constant background sound as our windows raised to let in a little more air, however warm.

Mom and Dad were first-generation American and spoke only English. Polish, Ukrainian, Hebrew, German, Italian, and Spanish were spoken only in the comfort of one's own home. We little library girls didn't understand the words as tone and pitch escalated, via the echoes of Busy Body Alley. We guessed the mood and often mimicked their words with strange sounds and other distortions. Other languages were alien to our world.

Mom didn't like us eavesdropping and making fun of others. She also didn't like nosey neighbors. A few times while Mom was hanging clothes, a curious tenant across the alleyway on the 11th Street side called out to her, "Isn't that the library?"

Mom answered with little to say but, "Yes, it is." She didn't give information freely when it came to our apartment and reminded us, "The less you say, the better." We did get a washing machine at Tompkins Square but no dryer until we moved to the Staten Island branch where there were no alleyways or clotheslines across from our library windows, only a view of New York Bay.

Wednesday was Dad's suit and tie day. He was on stair duty early afternoons, when school got out. I knew important men wore suits to work every day. Dad stood watch, calling out to the wild ones, "Don't run! Walk." He clearly spoke in a deep, quiet voice, "This is a library. No talking!"

Most of the children knew the quiet rule and obeyed it. Some boys liked to act out. So, the privilege of remaining in the public library, disturbing the readers and others, meant Dad had to do his job and throw them out with a warning, "Don't come back until you can behave. Obey the sign when you first come into the vestibule." Then a little louder, he would command, "Quiet."

Some of my elementary school friends would ask me in school, "What does your father do when he stands on the stairway?"

With pride, I would answer, "He kicks out stupid boys who run around and giggle."

Dad was respected at the local schools, and parents in the neighborhood knew when their children were at the library, they had to behave, or they might not be allowed to watch the Saturday morning cartoons. He would not entertain children who didn't behave but once the cartoons played, most of the children laughed and sat mesmerized.

Dad showed the reel-to-reel cartoons and documentaries, sometimes in other branches around New York City. He knew how to troubleshoot and fix the equipment if something went wrong. Dad was their behind-the-scenes man. This was an NYPL extra job for pay, and Dad truly enjoyed showing the films in both Tompkins Square and St. George branches.

My first memory of being different, a library girl, was the trip upstairs to my apartment at Tompkins Square. A sign that said, "Private," was posted at the entrance to the wide marble staircase to our third-floor apartment. New librarians and hired high school students in the summer months stopped us, "This is the children's room. You are not allowed upstairs."

One of us would approach the desk, mortified, and whisper, "We're Mr. Mitchell's daughters."

We then ducked under the heavy hanging black iron chain, and the two pedestal signs that warned "Private" and "No Admittance."

Helen, the oldest, remembers the only time Mom and Dad needed her to baby sit. She recalled an emergency meeting our parents had to attend at the main branch. That day the library was closed.

Helen was instructed to take care of her baby sisters. She recalled her duty, "Dad told me what to do in case there was an emergency. First, I had to keep your coats and hats out, ready just in case there was a fire in the library. I was absolutely petrified. I proceeded to instruct you and Irene to sit at the kitchen table, ready to leave from the third floor in case of a fire, making sure we had our coats with us. I checked all the exits and opened the door to the library staircase, just in case, so I could see flames or smell smoke first. I was in charge and at the ready. I told you and Irene that the fireman knew we lived in the library, but I wasn't really sure."

The Banquet Room was on the top floor next to our apartment. There were a few intruding pillars standing like they were on all the floors. Helen took piano lessons on Sundays. Afterward, Irene and I joined her riding our bikes and roller skating. Dad even set up a ping pong table for us.

There were a few tumbles. Once while I was learning to ride the two-wheeler bike, I hit the support pillars a few times and fell off. I didn't report the bruises. Helen and Irene and I never told, unless we had an open wound. Then Mom had to take care of the dressings. We kept this at mum's the word, or we'd lose our freedoms.

When Irene fell off the ladder, which the painters left out before a weekend, she fell off from the top, hit her head, then fainted. Dad took her to the hospital. She pulled through without major injury but that was a real game changer as we had a little less freedom in the Banquet Room.

Dad had a little hobby of his own. Spinning tops and doing tricks with one or sometimes two at a time. The top was a cylindrical wooden pear-shaped colorful toy with a steel point like a modern-day yoyo. With the flip of his wrist, a twist of his body, he concentrated on balancing the top as it magically moved up and down along the slender string. Sometimes he would flip it upwards resulting in a perfect landing back onto the thin string. With mastery, Dad was in total control of the spinning, all its movements. Sometimes he would do a 360 while the top was in the air and then catch it. "Timing is everything," Dad said often.

He bought new tops, more colorful ones at Jack's candy store at the corner of Avenue B. Jack made the best egg creams in the city. Egg creams seemed to wipe away the sweat from our brows and perhaps in that sense they were not only delicious but medicinal too.

Lasagna was our favorite Sunday dinner. We might have chicken soup with noodles, or dad's favorite, stuffed cabbage. Everything was home made. Mom started the Italian sauce the night before and simmered it for a long time. Hams and roasts were simmered for a few hours while we attended Sunday mass. Tradition of home cooked meals, church, and early lunch followed us to the St. George Branch in Staten Island. After lunch, we washed and dried the dishes, (no dishwasher), then we were back at playing around the library. Dad read the Sunday papers from cover and cover and Mom did some sewing or reading. In that sense, we epitomized an American Norman Rockwell family portrait.

We enjoyed everything from a game of hide and seek to playing tag, listening to "spooky" stories on the radio, and scaring each other in between riding our bikes around the support pillars, ducking and steering around the tables, down the narrow paths between stacks of books, racing around the spotless linoleum floors. We believed in ghosts who we were sure didn't come out to taunt us unless the library was closed. For all we knew, ghosts came out of books or from an old country map in the geography section. Sometimes we heard creaky floor footsteps with no one visible.

We would look around and then scare each other, "Did you hear that?" ..." What?" ... "That sound." Or, "I hear footsteps."

Then we would run upstairs, two steps at a time, and out of breath, huffing and puffing. We would tell Mom and Dad, screaming loudly, "There's a ghost downstairs, someone is walking around." Dad assured us there were no ghosts and that it was probably the wind. He'd quote from Teddy Roosevelt, "There's nothing to fear but fear itself."

When Dad was in his workroom, we felt safe enough to ride our bikes in the basement.

Helen's Sweet Sixteen birthday party was probably the biggest bash we ever had before we moved to the Staten Island branch. It was held in the Banquet Room.

Mom baked a big cake and we decorated with balloons and signs. Helen's Ukrainian boyfriend, Milku, and his friends dressed like bikers in black leather jackets with the stiff leather collar standing straight up, white T-shirts, and slicked back hair going from head to neck. The look signaled rebellion, a tough exterior. New neighborhood gangs in the 1950s emerged around the lower east side of Manhattan. The

Me and Dad dancing the Lindy at Helen's sweet sixteeth party

Ukraine boys were our defenders James Dean style. "Jailhouse Rock," was the biggest 45 LP hit. Rock and Roll was here to stay.

Helen made her debut wearing red lipstick, a pretty necklace, white satin blouse, black taffeta skirt, and black high heels. Photos snapped and flashes went off like lightning strikes. She was grown up as far as I was concerned.

Helen had a model's figure and looked as exquisite as Audrey Hepburn while Irene came in looking like actress Ann Bancroft with her big dark brown eyes, intelligence, and pretty face. I was Ginger Rogers in the making. We danced the day away with relatives and friends. In the evening, Helen, Irene, and her teen pals got their privacy in the Banquet Room without me. When the slow records began to play the young couples danced, and we left them alone.

I couldn't wait to be sixteen! At the time, I didn't know I would celebrate my sixteenth birthday party on a beach on the South Shore of Staten Island.

When Alfred Kinsey's first reports came out in the 1940s and early 1950s, there were lots of whispers about them. These reports contained a series of sexual history interviews. When released to the NYPL, the book was hidden behind the main desk counter (under lock and key) as "Adults only, Reference." Due to the nature of the book, it was not placed in the general reference area. Helen found out about the salacious special reference book. She and Irene planned on checking it out once Mom and Dad were not home and the library was closed.

I swore not to tell Mom and Dad about their expedition that weekend when my sisters found the key and opened that drawer. I asked them why I couldn't see the book. They just said I was too young to understand it. I remember each of them giggled a lot when I asked them if it was good! And neither of them said a word about its contents.

Sex was now out in the open, open for the entire neighborhood to read Kinsey's Report. I wonder now if anyone, other than Helen and Irene, who surreptitiously read it, asked a librarian to unlock the hidden book. Many researchers today said that Dr. Kinsey went too far into taboos and that perhaps Dr. Kinsey himself may have been a pedophile, based on his taboo research on incest.

I conclude the NYPL librarians knew their patrons at that time might not have been ready for the Kinsey reports. American families didn't discuss sex and when they did it was not in detail. I wonder what the librarians would have thought had they found out my sisters, Helen and Irene, read quite a bit of the Kinsey Reports.

The Impressionable Years

It was 1952. The United States was in a continued cold war with the Soviet Union, Harry Truman was president, my Uncle Al was at the 38th Parallel during the Korean War, and Herman Wouk won the Pulitzer Prize for fiction for his war story *The Caine Mutiny* soon to become a movie. And some time during that year I would be cast in the film, *The Impressionable Years.*

Films were a big event, just like theater. We looked forward to going to the movies once a week on Dad's day off. I fell in love with movie stars like Lucille Ball, Ann Francis, Judy Garland, Jane Powell, Debbie Reynolds, Barbara Stanwick, Liz Taylor, and Jean Simmons. My favorite nonfiction movie that year was *Jane Froman's Life Story* with Rita Hayward. I memorized the words to the hit song, "With a Song in My Heart." Froman was a singer, who was crippled in a plane crash yet made a heroic comeback. She sang for troops during World War II and fell in love with a navy pilot. Such drama was a tear-jerker for a young girl!

In 1952, word got around that the NYPL was about to make a documentary film of its own. It was to go around the world to every library. There was a lot of excitement generated, especially among the NYPL employees who had young children.

The film director was looking for an actress around six to eight years old. Dad came home one evening excited that auditions would be at the main branch. The librarians at our branch, Tompkins Square, told Dad he had to send their little library girl, me, to audition for the part. I was in the perfect age range. All librarians were excited about the audition. They cheered me on that day, "Carolyn, we hope you get the main role. Good luck!"

My imagination took me places I would never have thought possible! Imagine me in a film that would travel to every corner of the world's libraries. I would play the starring role. Then I could be discovered by a Hollywood producer just like famous actress Lana Turner, who was discovered in a California soda shop. She was only sixteen years old so I had the next eight years to learn how to act. I would audition, and Mom could tell them all about my experience.

I had performed as a ballerina in Swan Lake at the Christadora House on Avenue B about two years before. I won second place in Little Bo Peep contest at Tompkins Square Park, and I hoped Mom would not forget to tell them I got the lead role at camp for Rudolph the Red-Nosed Reindeer, which I couldn't perform because I got poison ivy; and I wondered if getting a photo with the Roller Derby at Tompkins Square Park might matter.

The auditions were held at the NYPL Main Library on 42nd Street. I sat on a bench, which I believe was the opening scene of *The Impressionable Years.* I didn't have to speak or memorize anything. We understood there would be a narrator as the girl wanders through the NYPL branches. Throughout the film, the girl star walks into book signings, picks up a book of her own, and opens a new library card. This recollection is from my memory of the filming so many decades ago.

In one scene, the star happens upon a gathering of children listening to the poetry of Carl Sandburg, a folk musician too, as he played a ukulele or banjo. Carl Sandburg won three Pulitzer Prizes, two in poetry, one on Abe Lincoln. He was also honored by the Poetry Society of America with a Gold Medal for Distinguished Achievement.

I didn't get the main role but was excited to be in one scene right in my own Tompkins Square Library. Mr. Sandburg was no stranger to showing up at many libraries. He was an entertainer, loved children, and wrote many books.

My family and the librarians were disappointed that I didn't get the main role, but the smaller role was the most important scene. I concluded, it was the best part, playing me.

In my scene, I joined a group of children at our branch. We listened intently to the famous poet, a good-looking fellow, with movie star ratings and an author who won many prizes for literature.

It was the best few minutes of the entire film, I am sure. I remember that childhood moment, what I wore, and my total immersion into Sandburg's aura. My eyes opened wide as I watched filmmakers who said, "Look into the big lens and act natural."

Carl Sandburg signing books, courtesy of NYPL Digital Collections

Several librarians prepared for the scene. Dad placed the children's room chairs in the area, and Mr. Sandburg was tuning his instrument as he smiled at the children present. There was a lot of film equipment and cameras ready to roll. Everyone scrambled around to add the final touches of magic. I was called into the reading group by one of our Tompkins Square librarians. About to take a back seat, I heard a commanding voice, "Where's Mr. Mitchell's library girl, Carolyn?" Carl Sandburg said with a smile and a deep voice. "Hello, Carolyn, do you like poetry?"

My favorite poem was "If" by Rudyard Kipling. I smiled and said, "Yes." I don't know if the camera was rolling yet.

He then asked, "Can you sit on my lap while I tell everyone here a little story about my farm?" (I found out later that he moved to his new home, a farm in North Carolina, 1952.)

When the filming began for my scene, everyone was quiet. People were crowding in to get a close look as the filming began. Dad handled the crowds. Sandburg tuned his ukulele and chose me to sit on his lap while he read "Buffalo Bill" and "Chicago" from his books of poetry. The cameras rolled, and I have one visual in my mind of that scene. I looked at him being so close-up and knew I was in the presence of a down to earth man despite his fame as a folk singer/author. He was a storyteller.

Sandburg enjoyed entertaining—reading and singing for children and did so quite often around libraries and at his farmhouse, now a national historic site in North Carolina. He made himself at home in the libraries of America.

In the 1960s, some fourteen years later, when we lived at the St. George Branch in Staten Island, Dad tried to obtain the film. He was told the film was in a state of disrepair, and the reel was not available. We were told that the entire section of the film with Carl Sandburg's poetry reading was cut out because that part of the tape had to be spliced due to fraying.

Sandburg at his estate in North Carolina, courtesy of NYPL Digital Collections.

We assumed that the trips it made around the world no doubt killed the footage. In those days, films had to be carefully stored and to preserve them was a monumental task. Even poor ventilation could destroy the best of Hollywood films. We were sad to hear it.

Upon doing some research for this memoir, I tried again to find out if any of the film had been salvaged. I found out from the reference librarian in the Moving Image Section of the Library of Congress in Washington, D.C., that the film existed. That librarian then referred me to the reference librarian at the NYPL Main Library. Within a few days she located it for me. Technology may have had a hand in putting it all together, miraculously.

I found out that the St. George Staten Island branch librarians were right at the time. The film was in a state of nonrepair. However, I got a pleasant surprise. The NYPL research librarian wrote me an email stating that two versions of the film had been restored. One is 40 minutes, with Carl Sandburg (with me, hopefully); the other version is 30 minutes without Carl Sandburg at Tompkins Square Branch. It was restored by New York University's Tisch School of Arts and not too long ago found its way to the archives of the New York Public Library for the Performing Arts at Lincoln Center, Dorothy and Lewis B. Cullman Center at 40 Lincoln Center Plaza. The Performing Arts Center opened in 1971.

Coincidentally, I used that new Library for the Performing Arts for a Renaissance Medieval Dances Project in my senior year of college. I loved going there. Next door is the Metropolitan Opera House and in the same square, the David Geffen Hall (Avery Hall in 1974) where I would one day perform.

The Impressionable Years influenced my life and the story of Carl Sandburg and me on his lap was a kitchen table story throughout the years, even as recently as the writing of this memoir. With thanks to a new class of filmmakers who took the challenge to restore this piece of history, I couldn't be happier that its new home is at the Lincoln Center Library for Performing Arts.

I often wondered over the decades how many countries had a presentation of *The Impressionable Years.* Was it narrated in other languages? I'll find out on my next visit to New York City. Or, ask a research librarian.

Tompkins Square Park and Historic Tompkins Square District

Just living is not enough, one must have sunshine, freedom, and a little flower.

—HANS CHRISTIAN ANDERSON

Tompkins Square Park has a history spanning over two centuries. It has been torn down, neglected, and revived time after time, war after war, century after century. Across from Tompkins Square Library, the Tompkins Square Park has a special name, the Historic Tompkins Square District. It is named after New York's Daniel D. Tompkins, who was governor from 1807 to 1817.

In 1811, Governor Tompkins bought parcels of land to be designated parks throughout the five boroughs of New York City. Tompkins Square Park was ten acres. The area offered immigrant families a place for social gatherings, events, and a playground for children.

The lower east side is where immigrant families first planted their American roots leaving the old country behind. My maternal grandparents were one of those families. Mom and my aunts and uncles were born on East 10th Street and First Avenue.

Thompkins Square Park concert, 1910, courtesy of NYPL Digital Collections.

After Tompkins Square Library became a landmark in 1999, the Tompkins Square Park followed in 2001. In 2012, the 10th Street block from Avenue A to Avenue B, its tenements, and standing brownstones were set in perpetuity as Tompkins Square Historic District. With this new designation came the rule that no renovations, additions, or facia changes outside the guidelines written by the New York City Landmark Preservation Commission.

Alongside the sidewalk of East 10th Street, where Tompkins Square Branch stands tall in the middle of the block, there were Cherry Blossom trees, flowering shrubs, even daffodils, rose and mulberry bushes.

I was born a decade after Saul Kovner painted this scene. Trees decorated the periphery and inside of the park. We had tall oaks, elms, and maple trees. They gave us shade in the hot summer, and, a signal that winter was fast approaching once the fallen autumn leaves blew away.

We made art from mother nature's leftovers, every season. By the end of winter's icy storms and blizzards, we couldn't wait for spring's Easter eggs, birds, bees and buds. All these weather changes returned, like an old welcome friend.

Whatever the season, our park taught us valuable lessons. We shared chalks with friends for sidewalk art and played games: tag, hide and seek, card games, like Old Maid. Strict rules were to be obeyed when it came to scores.

We had a ballfield, tennis, basketball, and softball areas, the wide-open spaces of country within the city. There was something for every age group.

Helen remembered her favorite places, "The first place I ran was to jungle gym, and, the swings. Mom sat on the benches, usually socializing with other mothers. Dad pitched balls and taught us how to catch and pitch. Some days we walked to Washington Square Park or rode the train uptown to Central Park for ice skating in the winter and row boating in the spring. The city had beaches in all the boroughs. We went to all of them on Dad's free days to cool off."

Thompkins Square Park, 1934 by Saul Kovner, courtesy of the Smithsonian American Art Museum.

Currier and Ives, Winter Pastime, 1855.

In winter, the boys threw snowballs like they were pitching hard balls. Sleds came out of the tenement apartment closet as soon as the neighborhood heard a big snowstorm was coming. Parents warned of "frostbite." We were instructed if we felt a tingling or numbness in our hands and feet, it was time to quit and go home. Snow days were the essence of exuberance, especially when businesses and schools closed. The city sparkled all on its own with the pristine first few inches before man's shoe prints planted the first human footsteps. New York City parks canvased a new coat of white.

Central Park was a destination for ice skating on the pond. We put on the mittens and ran toward the ice. There was work involved before joining other skaters on the rink. First the tug of war to get our feet into the skates then lacing the laces tight against the ankle. Mom looked on because she didn't skate and was happy for a little alone time. Dad was an excellent skater who showed off his figure eights, which he performed effortlessly.

Across the street from our library apartment, Tompkins Square Park, we built our snowman, every snowstorm. It lasted for a few days if very cold and no kids vandalized it. My sisters and I admired the workmanship of other snow architects, who built bridges and tunnels to crawl through for those who dared. Though the ice or snow sculptures were short lived, it was living in the moment that mattered. We built Frosty with a carrot nose, button eyes, Dad's old pipe, and an old scarf. Usually when everything melted, the scarf was the only proof Frosty once lived. We had no photo proof, only red cheeks, laughter, and a good appetite afterward while Mom made hot cocoa as we defrosted our fingers and toes.

The Currier and Ives outdoor scenes in mid-nineteenth century consisted of lively landscapes of American life from the Mississippi to the wild west. Some showed New York City horse and carriages from the Battery downtown to Central Park and the Hudson River and the countryside homes and churches. This was our city, steeped in tradition, almost perfect, a happy place.

At the park, we roller skated and rode our bikes through and around the little pathways, some very narrow, others along the main cut off. There were areas where old men sat to play chess and checkers. Concrete game tables had boards carved into them. Ladies strolled past with baby carriages, and sometimes a stray ball might fly by. There was always something going on in the park.

The Ninth Street cut-off sloped downhill at the mid-point section, between Avenue A and Avenue B. Learning to ride a bike could be treacherous because the hill was steep enough to pick up speed and lose control of the handlebars. Tumbling in a skirt was no fun either when the bike ran right into one of the brick posts the entrance/exit. It was about the same with roller skates. After some tears and bruises, followed by confidence, I got a little instruction from my big sisters. Helen and Irene gave me applause when I learned any sport, as did Mom and Dad, when they were able to join us.

Me, Dad, Irene and Helen on the red bike we won at the church bazaar, now our second bike.

I was too young to remember the event, but I heard the story many times. When I was only four years old,

Dad took me for a ride on our bike. He seated me on the back metal seat and told me to hold on to him and keep my feet up. "Hold on tight, ready?" I guess I forgot to keep my feet up.

Dad's version went like this, "Your foot got stuck in the spoke. I ran with you in my arms over to Dr. N's brownstone at the corner of 10th Street. You screamed and cried so loud I was sure your foot was broken. I hugged you and wiped those tears away. I felt so bad."

On another park day, Helen cracked her tooth at the water fountain. When she went to drink from the fountain, a girl from her school pushed her accidentally. That required a visit to the dentist and a root canal. Irene was upset the girl was careless, and with some certainty suggested, "She just shoved her. I saw it and I got mad."

I took my first ballet lessons at Christadora House, located directly across the street from the park. The lessons cost a quarter per class. Helen was the only one available to drop me off and pick me up two hours later. Two teen gangsters stole my quarter at the front door, shortly after she left. Tears welled up because I couldn't pay. The teacher allowed me to practice anyway for our Swan Lake performance that coming weekend. That incident changed everything.

My parents said it was too dark to be out at night with the teen gangs forming, so my ballet classes ended after the performance. I practiced solo in the library on the weekends where I could listen to records and learn ballet positions. I read about ballerinas Anna Pavlova and Margot Fonteyn. They influenced my love for dance. I watched Marge and Gower Champion, Gene Kelly, and Ann Miller, and the modern dancers like Isadora Duncan and Martha Graham.

My friends Frances, Mary Ann, and I would walk past St. Bridget's Church often when going into the park or exploring the neighborhood around the lower east side. We always made the sign of the cross, just in case. As Frances said, "If we die tomorrow, we'll go to heaven."

St. Bridget's was our parish church. Mom made sure we never missed a Sunday mass. This meant dressing up on Sunday morning. Church services and communion was our runway, where all the pretty outfits of parishioners competed for attention. The ladies wore the dead sable around their necks; mink faces with sad, dark eyes pointed downward.

There were hats made of straw with plastic berries, cherries, and flowers. Mom had a kelly-green picture hat, the brim so wide that when the sun shined through the open floral design, it left shadows on her face. Everyone enjoyed the fashions. The men were in suits and ties, and children dressed in the finest fanciest outfits. Mom made all our outfits. The only outfit Mom didn't make was my white communion dress.

The park was a popular place for photos especially after Sunday church, a birthday or holiday. Photos were also taken at the beach, weekends, and special occasions. Roller skating was a popular sport around town. Our skates, however, took a considerable amount of work to get into. First, we had to slide our street shoe into the steel heel foot enclosure then lock it in place. A skate key tightened the metal clamps over the front part of each shoe. The final step was to pull a strap over the shoe mid-point and buckle it. We wore the keys around our necks. When the metal steel clamps had to be unlocked, we needed the key at the ready. Mom said that while we were growing so fast, it would be expensive to buy the fancy skates every year and we might not use them again. The pro skaters used beautiful white leather skates and I wanted a pair as soon as I grew up.

Tompkins Square Park, my First Communion with Mom after church service.

One special day in 1950 was filled with excitement at Tompkins Square Park. The roller derby skaters who had recently won a World Series came to the city to perform at the park. They showed us how to perform more complicating skating, like backward, figure eights, turns, and leg extensions.

The ladies were beautiful and sweet and looked like athletes. We didn't have

Me, far right, at the New York Journal-American *Skating Derby, 1950*

too many women athletes in the early fifties. I couldn't believe that they wore white skates like ice skates. The only difference was they had wheels instead of blades. The men wore black skates up to the ankle.

I became a true feminist that very day when I complained about young girls wearing skirts for athletics. Too many knee scrapes and mercurochrome which burned. It wasn't long after that we girls bought our first blue jeans with red flannel lining and cuffs. Those were our first pants and we couldn't wait for Saturdays to wear them.

I didn't know that day that I would be asked to pose with the skaters for a newspaper photo, which landed on the front cover of the *New York Journal-American*. I was starstruck in the company of these professional skaters. I picked up my skirt a little to show a scraped knee. I began to understand that girls did not have the same privileges as boys.

The librarians pinned up the clipping onto the library notice board. Library staff mentioned it to me whenever they saw me. My relatives all bought the newspapers that day. Dad ordered a reprint photo. It was a big deal to get your photo in a newspaper. Mom heard some chatter at Busy Body Alley too. A few of the chatterboxes yelled out across the alley, "Was that your daughter in the newspaper Mrs. Mitchell?"

Mom answered with pride and a big smile, "That's my youngest one."

Orchard Beach, Manhattan Beach, Jones Beach, and the Rockaways were our main car rides.

Irene remembers what she didn't like about the park, "In the summer, we had those sprinklers at Tompkins Square Park. I didn't enjoy getting wet because I wanted to go to the beach and swim."

The summers were filled with trips to the beach. We would pack lunch for the trips on a hot summer weekend. Irene would swim out deep into the ocean while Dad gave me lessons. Mom relaxed. We had zucchini with onions on white bread or eggplant. Dad always treated us to ice cream. The man dressed in white, trudged through the sand, calling out, "Ice cream." Dad had to run to catch up.

Irene became our best long-distance swimmer and most closely resembled the Aqua water dancers in grace and form, and she was a good diver. Her technique was perfected from early years to adulthood.

On weekends, Dad drove us to Queens to see the Aqua Dance swimmers. It was an outdoor extravaganza. The swimmers dove into the pool and danced in synchronized formations. They were like the Ester Williams of the fifties, a champion swimmer and actress. Williams entertained us in film with her spectacular dives and bathing suit styles.

During vacation week from the library, Dad drove us to the Catskills where we spent time at lakes and swimming at the pool where we stayed for vacation. It's where Dad gave me my first swim lessons. He'd say, "Don't be afraid. I got you. Jump."

Aside from the wonderful trips we took to the botanical gardens and zoos, longer car trips to the Cloisters and to Croton's Dam always gave us something new to explore. It was what families in the fifties enjoyed doing together. They drove around on Saturdays and Sundays.

I cannot ever forget our trips to Calvery Cemetery in Queens, New York. We would visit Grandma Angelina Milo's gravesite. Together we planted morning glories, violets, and marigolds. And afterward, on the

Dad, Mom, Helen, Irene, and me, with Aunt JoAnne and Uncle Al

route to Grandpa's house, as we walked along the pathway back to the car, we studied the names and dates on the mausoleums. I thought it was best to be inside an enclosure rather than outside in dirt when it rained. Mom said we shouldn't have to worry about that for a long time. The cemetery had a parkside ambiance with beautiful flowers, winding paths, shading trees, and benches. It was a day out. First stop, Grandma's and then we drove to Grandpa's in the Hudson 1949 not far from the cemetery.

I would tell her about school and other things because she never met me. I was born only a few months after she went to heaven. Grandpa Steven didn't speak English, but he took us for walks around his garden. We picked vegetables and grapes for winemaking while the oxtail spaghetti sauce simmered.

I've drawn a pretty picture of my Tompkins Square neighborhood, our little family trips, and how we spent our free time.

That takes me to the good old Golden Rule Days of writing, reading, and arithmetic. A child's major obligation was to learn and get an education, which my parents didn't have the opportunity to get.

As I can remember it, it all began very early in the morning when Dad came up to join us for breakfast singing a popular old song written in 1912, "School days, school days, dear old golden rule days, readin' and ritin' and 'rithmetic, taught to the tune of the hick-ry stick."

Helen, Irene and me at Calgary Cemetery, Queens, New York

CHAPTER FOUR

School Days, P.S. 122
Lower East Side

You cannot open a book without learning something

—CONFUCIUS

SINCE THERE WAS THREE of us and only two bedrooms, Irene and I usually shared a bedroom. Helen got her own bedroom because she was the oldest. Cuddled in layers of blankets, early morning wake-up calls consisted of the sights and sounds of the radiator's tiny valve hissing like a tea kettle's whistle. A second later, a shot of streaming steam would burst into the room, adding more heat. Once I asked Dad why it made so much noise and told him I was afraid that the radiator might blow up.

Dad explained, "Heat goes straight upstairs, so it's the hottest first thing in the morning. When I grew up, sometimes we froze. Chicago was very cold."

Dad explained in person once when I witnessed the heat coming from the furnace down in the basement. He shoveled the coal into a small thick iron container. The sparkling black coal rocks transitioned from diamond-like beauties to roaring giants. Dad lifted me up to peek into the furnace and see the process for myself. The standing coals, once ignited, turned the brightest red and flickering orange color. They crackled and popped, igniting the fury of flying embers. As the small flames died down, ocean-like mirages of waves traveled across the hottest coals. Dad returned me to the floor, after my face flushed red.

Then came the warning, "Never come near the furnace without me, OK?"

In the morning Dad finished early duties, like stoking the coals and preparing to open the library. He often joined us for breakfast with a cheerful singing voice, "You gotta get up, you gotta get up in the morning."

When we three library girls attended grade school, our daily commute was different from that of our peers. Although early morning walks to school and returning home was routine, our lives were a little less ordinary. Can you imagine the people going to and from work or school passing our block who with curious eyes fixated upon three little girls leaving the library? The library opened a few hours after the morning rush hour. Getting ready for school began the night before when we laid out our favorite weather-appropriate outfits. Winters took more clothing, therefore, more planning for the morning commute to school.

Mom was strict about dressing for the weather. All bets were off if the radio weatherman described the day's outlook as cold, windy, or, God forbid, rain or snow was in the forecast. This disappointed three little girls when the fashionable outfits had to go back into the closet. Pretty shoes were replaced by "older shoes" or, even worse, the rubber raincoats and boots went on. The hats came out, pulled down over our ears. The gloves and mittens were secured.

Last, but by no means least, the pièce de résistance, intricately hand-woven woolen scarves were wrapped several times around each of our faces and mouths, leaving only about an inch of space, just enough for the nostrils to take in air!

Somedays, if it snowed hard enough, the announcements came through on the radio that there was no school. This was exciting news. What a treat it was to stay home and watch the snow fall then go play across the street at the park when it stopped and throw snowballs at each other. The park was covered over in white and the most spectacular warmth followed a big snowstorm.

When there was no news of school closings, my dreaded snowsuit came out. I screamed once the final zipper went up, and sometimes I'd win if I unpacked myself from the bottom pants. With the onset of tears trickling down my cheeks, I hoped to get my way. With tears I begged,

Me in my snowsuit.

"Mommy, I hate that snowsuit and I can't walk in it with my dress tucked inside. David B called me a boy last time I wore it because girls don't wear pants."

When she said to pay no attention to him, I explained the bitter truth, "I turned him in during a fire drill when the teacher asked who was making all the noise. His friends said I was a tattletale."

David followed me home the last time I wore that snowsuit, with a few giggly boys, saying I looked like a library girl in boy's pants. I didn't want to be bullied again. That day after school, the bullies entered the main floor of Tompkins Square and Dad happened to be on stair duty. When the boys saw him walking with authority toward them as they began to follow me up to the forbidden top floor, Dad took charge and grabbed two of the boys by the collar. He dragged them downstairs into the marble vestibule. I peeked down over the landing and noticed a little of the jostling but couldn't hear what Dad said. Let's just say I knew my Dad had power and I was grateful for it. The next day, David B said he was only kidding and that he liked me.

The walk to and from school was my oldest sister Helen's responsibility. She oversaw getting us to school safely. She took her responsibilities for her sisters seriously. Before crossing, she gave the orders, "Put your mittens back on or I'll tell mommy" or, "wait until the light turns green."

Irene would dutifully hold my hand or adjust my buttons and assist in putting the mittens back on I had already taken off. She clenched my hands tightly until Helen gave the order to cross the street. With the anticipation of a red light, Helen promptly gave the order, "Hold hands, the light is green. Let's go." We'd run for our lives across Avenue A!

Best wishes to a
little library girl.
Eliza Perry

greetings to Carol
Hurry up and get old
enough to work at Ts. I'll
think of you on June
26th.

Blanche Braunick

These were the perks being a baby sister—forgiveness, sheltering, nurturing, and protection by my big sisters, even in school. They picked me up in my classroom for the walk home for lunch. Mom always made us a home cooked meal. And then, at the end, she added a tablespoon of cod liver oil for good measure.

I found out quickly there were rules to follow and that whatever happened, the teacher was the authority during school hours once we library girls moved to our separate classrooms. It all began in kindergarten, which the moms referred to as *kinnygarten*. It would have been fun, except for the one boy who whined and never got to the bathroom on time. The teacher had to mother him.

Over the next few years I don't recall class activities, but I loved to write cursive. Helen and Irene had beautiful handwriting, but, mine was a little less artful.

School was like a little city of its own with its own rules. Some children had privileges, some had money, others didn't wear clean clothes, and mothers all dressed up in competition with their status quo. I was most fascinated with parents who "brown nosed" teachers and how skillful some kids were at becoming teacher's pet. Going from my loving home to an uncertain environment taught me the unwritten rules of society. My mom didn't care about getting involved in any of the parent-teacher meetings.

She said she was too busy with her family duties to be sitting around with the ladies and to commit to committees. Mom was a library girl too and felt her world was perfect the way it was with my dad, Helen, Irene, and me.

When my second-grade teacher said I daydreamed a lot, Mom counterpunched with, "I don't see anything wrong with daydreaming!"

I was happy Mom understood that I was a daydreamer, and it wasn't bad. If bored, I daydreamed mostly about dancing with Gene Kelly and Fred Astaire or what it would be like to wear lipstick or become a teenager and go out with friends.

The summer following second grade I joined my sisters at Northover Camp. I was in the little kids' campsite, Pipsissawah, and happy to join Helen and Irene, just to have them around made me feel safer. However, I remember the traumas more than the fun, like the time I came face to face with a snake when I picked up a bird's nest or the fellow camper who held my head under water until I nearly drowned. My big sisters took care of telling the counselors whenever I cried. The worst of days is when I lost the main role in a play, *Rudolph the Red-Nosed Reindeer* because I got poison ivy. I don't know why we were doing a Christmas show in summer, but that was the play.

The poison ivy spread over my chest, my face swelled up, and my eyes swelled closed. The camp nurse, Miss S, quarantined me. I thought she had locked me in a dungeon because I couldn't see. It was a little room, and I cried a river of tears until the nurse said no one would hear me and my Mom would come in the morning.

Miss S said Irene could not stay in quarantine. She snuck back in the cover of darkness and stayed the night, holding my hand until Mom came that next morning. She was so brave.

When we heard our own mother was hired as the head counselor, I was relieved. The rest of the summer was a breeze having my real-life guardian angel around. Dutifully, Mom painted the calamine lotion onto my face, like she did her powder, every morning.

I stayed with her and not my bunk. I looked like a monster with my swollen face. But my sisters and my mom kept me safe from ridicule. Mom heard the gossip that one of my fellow roommates spread the poison ivy leaf over my pillow but it was never confirmed.

To sum up summer camp, it wasn't any less stressful than going to school, but I was glad to get home to cement city. I don't remember much else until I entered the fifth grade. That was my best year in elementary school.

School was never fun, although Miss Z, my fifth grade teacher, was the exception. She was soft spoken, pretty, and sweet. She wore high heels and tight suits with plunging necklines. The biggest day in Miss Z's class was when she showed off her engagement ring. Her diamond ring was unlike anything I'd ever seen, bigger than Mom's and shinier

Miss Z, my fifth-grade teacher

than the North Star. It sparked prisms of light that reflected off her dark brown eyes when she stood near the room's floor to ceiling windows. The light burst into the classroom, even on rainy days. I felt safe with Miss Z, even loved. She was confident and classy. I looked forward to going to school for the very first time.

Miss Z brought gardenia and lilac hand lotions the first day and stored the bottles in her desk drawer. Every morning, she dutifully spread the cream around her red painted fingernails. Then with speedy resolve, all ten fingers and hands drank the magic potion before class began. Some days her nails were painted red, other days they might be pink. As the ritual began, and sensuous smells of gardenia or lilac filled the classroom air, boys giggled and pointed to her shapely legs as they'd strain to look below the hemline. Sometimes they made kissy sounds or passed notes back and forth. She ignored them but would address their antics, while she wrote on the blackboard, saying things in a calm serious low tone, "Boys, you may get in trouble if you don't pay attention."

Miss Z was strict about homework. Every other day, she would check to see who did a great job. This was a big part of the grades. Checking homework and grading it was a ritual and she said if we did the homework, everyone would get a passing grade.

She'd order us in a soft voice, "Please take out your homework."

She glided toward each desk, each child, looked at our work slowly and meticulously, checking each of our answers and penmanship. Her pointy patent leather high heels would click, like the sound of a slow-moving metronome. You could hear the click-clack of one heel in front of the other as she graded the assignment, "A, B, C, or Fail." Some zeros counted toward final grades. Then a call went to the parents. Now that was serious.

She made assignments seem like fun, so I put the extra effort in because I wanted to please her. Miss Z was my first teacher who didn't look or act like the nuns from St. Bridget.

When she learned I lived in the library on open school night, she told Mom and Dad, "It must be a wonderful place to live, and, that's why Carolyn is so smart."

Miss Z was the good fairy godmother, good to all her children, complimentary about her kids to the parents, even the ones who got zeros.

How could I have known Miss Z would be the calm before the storm, a hurricane named Miss B?

I moved into grade 6-1. My sisters both had Miss B, and everyone knew she was a tyrant. Irene said she had feared to speak in that class. Helen had been afraid to put her hand up to be excused for the bathroom. I got the worst of her and it was a rough year. I was the last of her library girls she tortured.

Sixth grade was my last year of elementary school prison. Things couldn't be more chaotic with this teacher. I wished I could stay home with my beautiful mom, but school attendance and learning were something most parents insisted on, and the law sent out truancy officers to the homes of those children who didn't show up. The truants were named and ridiculed at the school. In those days, early fifties, children were responsible for their own behavior.

Every Monday, I dreamed about the next holiday just to recuperate from the pressure the tyrant put on me each day. Holidays went by so quickly that there wasn't even time to rest from Miss B's rantings.

A part in Swan Lake at the local community center, Christadora House, was a favorite escape. And even catechism release on Wednesday afternoon was a break. The cranky nuns were easier to get along with, even though some were very strict and showed us no mercy if we dared get out of line, like laughing and having fun seemed off limits. A handy ruler sat on the nun's desk ready to smack any face showing signs of life.

One day at school, I was at the class blackboard and brought my notecards to copy an outline. After I finished, Miss B went to the blackboard and found that the cards had stamped on the back, "Property of the NYPL." She insisted the thief stand up. I never did but told my dad how scared I was. He said he'd talk to her about the benefits of living in the library and never wasting scrap paper or cards.

After Dad explained the NYPL cards, she yelled a little less, but her rage showed through her cracked yellow teeth. Those spinster-like laced up shoes didn't help either. Miss B was nothing like Miss. Z. My health and happiness declined that year. I tried to stay home but it didn't work.

At bedtime prayers I asked St. Therese, Little Flower of Jesus, to intervene with my ongoing battle with Miss B. I chose St. Therese because a shiny varnished wall plaque, perhaps it was decoupage, hung above my parents' bed. She looked like my Mom, Theresa. I asked to be invisible in the class. My answer came after a full year of praying. After graduation Miss B moved to the suburbs, far away.

She was the first sign that evil existed, and I knew she may not be the only one. Despite Miss B's threats that I would not graduate for some rule I had broken or turning my head at the wrong time, I did graduate though much thinner from the abuse. With Mom, Dad, and my sisters, Helen and Irene, by my side. I wore my St. Theresa gold medal necklace.

The last school I attended in the city was P.S. 60 Middle School. My closest friends were Frances A and Mary Ann M and my newest friend, Maria. She had immigrated from South America and spoke English well but with an accent. She was a Flamenco dancer and I wanted to learn the Spanish dance's intricate steps.

I first learned about a different culture through Maria. She performed a dance routine with castanets that clicked in perfect timing as her toes and heels tapped the wooden floor. Her skirt added flair to the composition as her waist long hair swirled around her movements. It was thick and black. How did she learn to be so good? Hers was a show of skill and beauty. I wanted to know everything about her life and her country.

I found out Maria had studied Flamenco dance from the age of two and she learned English from a tutor in South America, which I knew was a continent. I became fast friends with Maria. She fit right in with Frances, Mary Ann, and me. I couldn't wait for her to teach me how to use the castanets, but an unexpected path was to re-write my destiny.

It wasn't long after that first year of middle school that my life as an urban library girl would soon take a new direction, and I would never see my city friends again, even though I never forgot any of them.

Dad got a promotion and we moved to the Staten Island St. George Branch of the New York Public Library. It would be an adjustment to move to an entirely new borough where I knew no one. My sisters and I had each other, at least for a while.

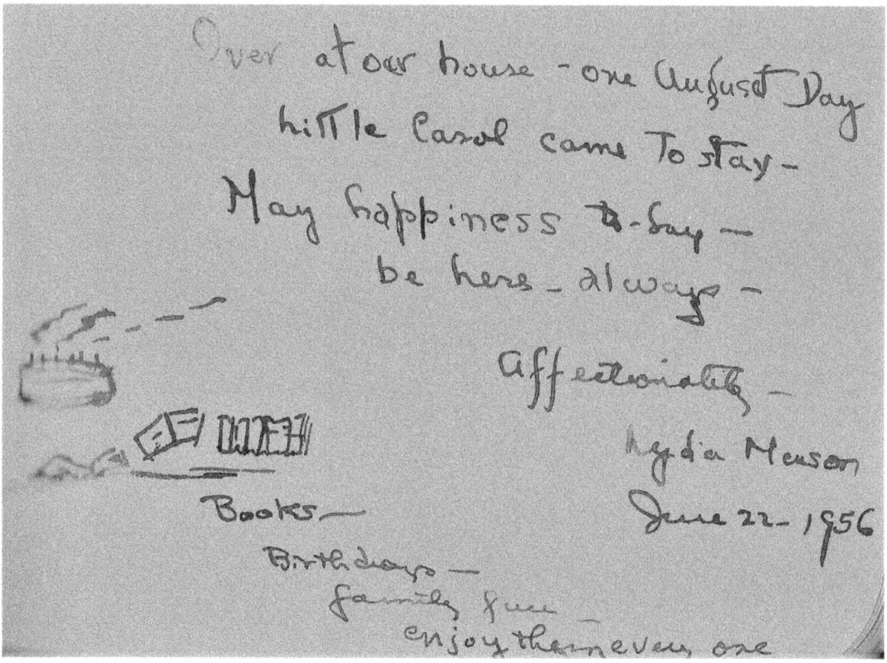
Over at our house - one August Day
Little Carol came to stay -
May happiness to-day -
be here - always -
Affectionately -
Lydia Mason
June 22 - 1956
Books -
Birthdays -
family fun -
enjoy them every one

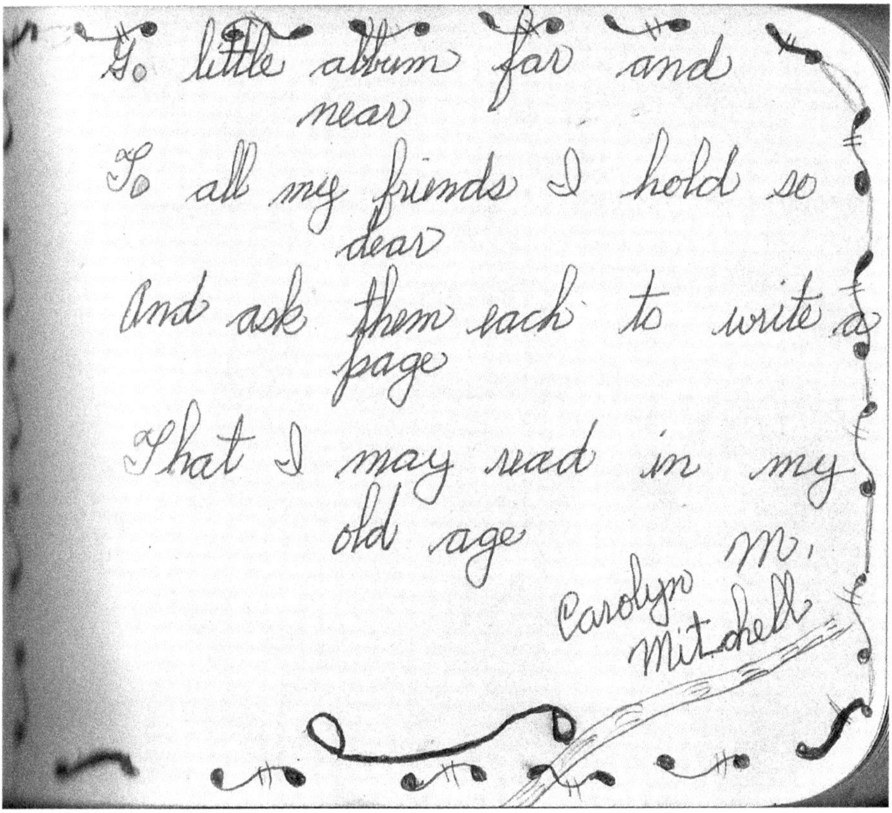
Go little album far and near
To all my friends I hold so dear
And ask them each to write a page
That I may read in my old age
Carolyn M. Mitchell

CHAPTER FIVE

St. George, Staten Island
New York City

I must go down to the seas again, to the lonely sea and sky.
—JOHN MASEFIELD

LONG AFTER MY DAD retired from the NYPL, the New York City Landmarks Commission dedicated St. George, Staten Island, as the St. George Historic District in 1994. The district from Hyatt Street to Stuyvesant Place includes Curtis High School and St Peter's Church, my parish. I remember the steeple, which stood prominently surrounded on St. Marks Place by Victorian homes. Also included are Borough Hall and the ornate St. George Theatre. Following the above-named landmarks, my second home, the St. George Public Library Branch was granted landmark status in 2003.

The St. George Branch was designed by Carrere and Hastings, the Beaux-Arts architects (1858–1911) who designed the palatial NYPL main branch, now named the Steven A. Schwartzman Building. Mr. Carrere was a long-time resident of Staten Island.

Sea Fever
John Masefield, 1902

I must go down to the seas again, to the lonely sea and the sky,
And all I ask is a tall ship and a star to steer her by;
And the wheel's kick and the wind's song and the white sail's shaking,
And a grey mist on the sea's face, and a grey dawn breaking.

I must go down to the seas again, for the call of the running tide
Is a wild call and a clear call that may not be denied;
And all I ask is a windy day with the white clouds flying,
And the flung spray and the blown spume, and the seagulls crying.

I must go down to the seas again, to the vagrant gypsy life,
To the gull's way and the whale's way where the wind's like a
whetted knife;
And all I ask is a merry yarn from a laughing fellow-rover,
and quiet sleep and a sweet dream when the long trick's over.

Sea Room, St. George, courtesy of NYPL Digital Collections

The Island
Staten Island, New York City

"All aboard!" A loud last call echoed through the terminal as passengers ran toward the closing doors leading to the Staten Island Ferryboat ramp. The trip began at downtown Manhattan's Whitehall Street slip with Wall Street in walking distance and giant skyscrapers overshadowing the waterfront docks. A crew member blew the horn as loud engines went into gear, churning up the foaming underbelly beneath us, engines full speed ahead. A short time after, we passed the Statue of Liberty, New Jersey coastline, and the Verrazano Narrows Bridge to Brooklyn. The final stretch sketched the steep hills of the North Shore of Staten Island. Within 25 minutes, the ferry docked on Staten Island's north shore, almost home. The skyline that we saw was noticeably changed when the 9/11 Twin Towers gave way to the new One World Trade Center.

Sunset, New York Harbor, courtesy of Topher Campbell

The smell of sea salt, the sights and sounds of birds of prey, seagulls, vultures, and pigeons were not necessarily the prettiest but certainly the best housekeepers. They eat crumbs from leftover pizzas, donuts, and hot dogs bought at the terminal food stands. Commuters' left-overs scattered throughout the boats were ravished by our usual trail of winged creatures who belong as much to the scenery now as they always had—as mother nature intended. Deep breaths in and out, this was my mantra whenever the ferry crashed against the pilings, tossing us about the deck. Commuters were only a few exhilarating breaths away from the next connection home.

Staten Islanders refer to their home as "The Island" with a sense of pride. It has been referred to as the forgotten borough despite its extensive history. The Lenape Nation Native Indian tribes came centuries before the first European settlers, the Dutch, who took up residency circa 1600 and named it Staaten Island. Over the decades Europeans populated the island. In 1964, shortly after I graduated from Curtis High School, the Verrazano-Narrows Bridge brought in many more residents after its construction.

I can imagine that those early settlers found a peaceful hide-a-way here. In the fifties and sixties, when I was a teenager, the Staten Island ferry was the only direct route in and out of the city, even for cars, which are no longer transported.

Tompkins Square was a familiar household name growing up on the lower east side, Tompkins Square Library and Tompkins Square Park. When I lived in Tompkins Square Library on East 10th Street, I didn't know anything about this American patriot, Daniel D. Tompkins.

Being the governor of the state of New York was not his only legacy. He was also vice president to James Madison. Tompkins lived on Staten Island and called it home. He was buried at St. Marks Church on the lower east side of Manhattan, not far from Tompkins Square Historic District.

Tompkins (1774–1843) bought several acres of farmland in 1812. It was known as the Village of Tompkinsville. He lived

Tompkinsville Ferry, retired to the ship graveyard, courtesy of Topher Campbell.

here until his death at age 51, leaving his estate to eight children. Tompkinsville is within walking distance of my library apartment in St. George and where my first school, P.S. 16, was located.

In 1817, shortly after Tompkins helped fund the War of 1812, he secured a charter through the Richmond Turnpike Company, to run a public ferryboat, Nautilus, from the city to Staten Island as the first mechanically "steamed" power boat and to add the first waterfront docks.

The view of Staten Island from the ferryboat held a sense of mystery. It would be a challenge and an adventure, a prescription my parents put forth as food for thought on the positives of moving.

Staten Island Ferry against lower Manhattan skyline, courtesy Robert E. Seeley, 2017

My parents suggested, "Think of moving to Staten Island as a new adventure."

For a 12-year old this advice was worthy of consideration, but none of us had a say in the matter anyway.

In the summer of 1957, Dad decided a move to the St. George Library would be a step up from the stresses of city life. Helen and Irene were already teenagers with strong ties to the big city before they each began college.

Helen and Irene got summer jobs. Irene worked at the New York Telephone Company and Helen worked corporate. During other months of the year, and at Tompkins Square, they worked as part-time library pages (clerks).

The first summer I acclimated to suburban life touring the island with Mom and Dad from shore to shore. Dad had just bought a used 1953 Plymouth. We walked the lake paths, which were a short distance from home. Silver Lake, which held the reservoir, and Clove Lakes had horse stables and bicycle paths, not crowded with city distractions, like Tompkins Square Park, where we had to navigate our bikes carefully so as not to hit anyone. The south shore was rural with yachts and beaches and restaurants overlooking New York Bay. Summer breezes were cooler than in the city.

Eventually, we got a window air conditioner when we moved to the St. George Branch. It cooled the living room, our gathering place for family night television and company.

St. George Public Library

The main entrance to the library is on Hyatt Street. We had our own entrance door going from the apartment hallway to the children's room. From there I could get to the main floor adult section.

St. George Library Main Entrance, Hyatt Street, courtesy NYPL Digital Collection

Entrance to library apartment from the children's room, courtesy of NYPL Digital Collections

Sunday was the day I went through magazines, listened to records, and worked on homework research assignments. Sometimes a friend stopped by, usually Marian and Sigrid. It was the one day the library closed, and we did homework in the library together.

During the week, I took my library card and notebook, used the short cut through the children's room to get into any floor of the library. Like Tompkins Square Branch, staff members looked up cautiously. I knew that look, so I identified myself, "Hello, I'm Carolyn, Mr. Mitchell's daughter."

The children's room (located on the Central Avenue side) offered a museum-like ambiance of merchant ships held within glass cases; some artfully placed inside bottles, even along the top shelf bookcases, not within reach. Paintings or lithographs were hung well above for enlightenment throughout the library. Dad made many of the frames using the craftmanship skills he had honed at the Tompkins Square Branch.

The architects of the St. George Branch, Carrere and Hastings, knew what they were doing when they chose to place many windows and glass doors overlooking the harbor view. In the children's room on a sunny day, light passed through the multicolored tall stained-glass windows reflecting a rainbow of prisms onto the cathedral ceilings, spilling out onto the side walls.

Our apartment had plenty of windows but none with stained glass. However, we adored our bedroom French door windows which opened to the inside. A screen kept any insects out.

The Sea Room and the harbor view were a perfect setting for a daydreamer. Dad read his Sunday papers while at the same time he kept an eye on a roast or ham cooking in the oven. Mom and her library girls went to church every Sunday. We walked past the Victorian homes along St. Marks Place to attend mass at St. Peters, the oldest of 36 Roman Catholic churches on the island. It was the same walk I took to Curtis High every day.

The St. George Library apartment had two floors. There was a private entrance on Central Avenue, where the path led to our front door and the steps down to Hyatt Street. The Library opened in 1907. We arrived 50 years later into this Carnegie live-in library.

St. George Library (now named St. George Library Center) showing the side entrance to our apartment

Our apartment living room windows showcased a parade of vessels and seascapes of many-colored skies depending on the weather and the time of day or night. On foggy mornings we could hear fog horns but see very little ahead, which usually meant a boat might be running late.

Irene commented, "I usually looked out the living room window to see how far the next ferry boat was from docking and then run for it, all the way down the library steps, then fly down the hill, making sure the nickel was ready for the turnstile!" (Now the ride is free.)

Once Dad bought binoculars it was much easier for us to spy on a vessel and spot stars in a clear night sky. Irene used them to calculate her trip to the ferry terminal more efficiently.

My cubby nook was perfect for watching the bay's changing scenes, the motion of frothing white-tipped waves, and the sky's coloring book painted day into night. A volatile waterway of heavy currents brought dolphins, whales, and other sea creatures frolicking above the waves. Having a front row view to so much nature sharpened the imagination. This tiny crawl-in space was meant for pondering and a little poetic line jotted down here and there.

The second attic bedroom looked over onto the Central Avenue side. We had a clear view of the marquee of the St. George Theater. At the top of the Hyatt Street hill stood a steepled church. Directly across from Central Avenue, a vacant lot would soon become a parking lot.

A good mystery stirred up the imagination, especially for an adolescent closet writer, me, and her friends. Ann, Joan, Marian, Sigrid, Pam and I discussed all the possible clues that we were not alone in the universe.

There were reports of unexplained phenomenon from pilots who reported "entities" unexplained during a flight. I once read that a B-17 bomber during World War II landed itself, without even one soldier on board. Once it was recorded that an alien spaceship with bodies crashed in Roswell, New Mexico, while many other sightings have been documented. I was sure one of us might see something if we kept on it, even a ghost.

Best friends remembered my library apartment and often one spent the night. The trips downstairs when the library was closed held special memories. Marian recalled recently, "We heard sounds and thought ghosts resided inside the library. We went to explore where the sounds came from. It was quite a good time being scared to death. We looked behind hidden corners around bookshelves. We were sure the library was haunted. I looked forward to your library apartment invitations."

Adjacent to the cubby nook, under the slanted wall of our attic ceiling was a big oak desk that Dad made for his college girls (Helen and Irene) in his St. George Library workroom. Dad's workroom was downstairs, very close to our apartment. The oak desk was varnished in a blond color and had six deep drawers that both of my sisters had a key to unlock. The gold ornate handles were well crafted. There were two hidden writing shelves, one on each side, which could easily be pulled out for extra writing space. There was an old 1940s black typewriter sitting in the corner and an inkwell.

Nowadays, Irene, a published lyric poet, continues to pen her books of poetry at this desk, now in her home. I believe she kept the heavy Merriam Webster desk dictionary with many thousands of words and hundreds of pages and photos. The librarians gave us the old ones when they got the newest edition.

A museum piece, a work of art, Dad's desk stood the test of time. The craftsmanship could only be compared to the oak crib Dad made for my dolls in the old library workroom at Tompkins Square. Building us useful furniture was Dad's way of showing us how much we were loved and appreciated.

In dense fog or during a full-blown snowstorm, fog horns would ring out in the early morning, just in time to wake up to the same familiar sound the radiator made at our Tompkins Square apartment, hissing and clanging, and that final shot of steam.

Mom would ring her hand-held bell from downstairs to indicate we must get up for breakfast. Dad had the same 24/7 hours maintaining the St. George Branch. The routine wasn't much different from Tompkins Square. But his library girls were growing up.

Dinner wasn't the same gathering around the pink table, although the table came with us. At Tompkins Square's big kitchen, that table joined the five of us together every evening. At St. George, we had a smaller kitchen and ate at the pink table, located in the living room, only when we had company. When Helen and Irene began college, they joined a sorority at Hunter College, Alpha Gamma Delta. We didn't see much of either of them at dinner. They were now an elite class of college girls. Now, Mom, Dad, and I had dinner at the kitchen table. The leftovers waited for my sisters when they eventually returned from classes.

Living inside the largest library on Staten Island was a new challenge, even for Mom and Dad. For Dad he had three-floors and a basement to take care of and large stained-glass windows. Helen and Irene had a long trip to Hunter College. On the evening trip home, Irene sat outside to relax, enjoying sea breezes while Helen studied in the inside.

Hunter College was a train and a ferry boat ride away from Staten Island. It would take a little over an hour to get to Lexington Avenue and 68th Street, if all connections were made on time. I began the eighth grade before attending Curtis High School.

My path couldn't have been more different from Helen and Irene's all-girls Washington Irving High School on East 18th Street in the city. Both graduated with honors. I had a lot to look up to with my two successful sisters. They were about to change the world and the role women would play in it.

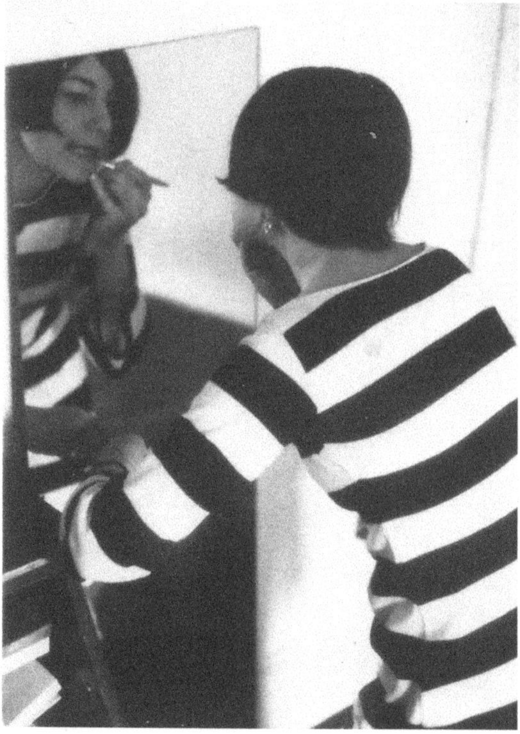

Sister Helen at Hunter College

My childhood memories of art were the arts and crafts we as a family created at home as well as the art surrounding us in New York City which was omnipresent. Every place a New Yorker looks, art is alive. It speaks to us from huge wall murals, museums, fashion, architecture, and within our beloved libraries.

In the fifties and into the sixties, paint-by-numbers kits were all the rage and our family loved them too. Helen painted the detailed canvases of Medieval and Renaissance court jesters and festive scenes. She painted well within the lines with a steady hand. Irene worked on the famous artists like Manet and Renoir, and I worked on the ballet dancers. Mom chose Picasso's Sunflowers and other still life paintings. We started painting the kits at Tompkins Square Branch and painted a few more while on the Island. Dad made all the frames for the completed sets or solos. All of us had a spotlight in the gallery wall of art.

The living room wall art was hung with signed artists alongside ours. In addition to a signed watercolor Dad bought at an art fair in Washington Square Park when we lived at Tompkins Square, there was a detailed embroidered Chinese silk peacock, quite large. Dad made a gigantic frame for it. He bought it from a Chinese restaurant owner in Hoboken, where we ate on Sundays after long drives to a New Jersey park or beaches. The owner's daughter embroidered it.

Ballerina paint-by-numbers

Mom admired the details, each carefully chosen thread of the peacock feathers, a tree of life and an orange sun. These were symbols of good fortune and happiness, the restaurant owner told us.

Today, the delicate silk embroidered peacock hangs on my wall, protected in a new frame and backing. Irene took the watercolor depicting Washington Square Park Arch in Greenwich Village. Helen took the wedding photo.

I like the memory of another pretty picture of home, my family masterpieces of art tucked away deep into my hippocampus, where miles of memories and emotions live. In such a tiny space, in my brain, are details of such moments, found and recorded, now an historic footprint. The paint-by-numbers masterpieces I warmly refer to are ripples of a past, ever present.

Curtis High School, The Castle

It seems they had been and would be friends.
Time could change, but not that.

—A. A. MILNE, WINNIE THE POOH

Eighth Grade Graduation, P.S. 16, back path of St. George Library leading to Hyatt Street

My first day of school at P.S. 16, Tompkinsville, was a day I have relived many times. There were beautiful faces who came to welcome me and escort me from the principal's office to my new classroom, Mr. D's 8-1 class. The welcoming committee, those friendly faces, smiled as brightly as twinkling stars. They accepted me with open arms, sharing tips about our teachers and warnings on what not to do. I fit right in—right into their lives for years to come. Nick became a Vietnam hero. After his death, his alma mater, Wagner College, placed a statue in his honor on campus. Tony joined the first passenger car to cross the Verrazano-Narrows

Curtis High School, courtesy of Staten Island Advance

Bridge to Brooklyn in 1964. Ramon became a pilot and school historian; Morty, a lawyer and musician; and Jay, a sportswriter. Ann, Carol, Joan, Marian, Pam, and Sigrid went on with me to successful careers as I found out at our 40th high school reunion in 2002. All of us married at some point.

It was time to pass the torch from my favorite fifth grade elementary school teacher (Miss Z) from the city to Mr. D, who prepared us for high school academically with a kind and loving heart.

Our Class 8-1 was well prepared when we entered Curtis High School with pen and notebook in hand. There were proms and dances, falling in and out of puppy love. It was exactly what it should have been—a place to mingle, learn, laugh, and cry as we moved along the four years. Our Castle, one of the top schools in the New York City area was academically competitive in the early 1960s.

We had two guidance counselors—one was sweet and kind, the other one only chose a few from our class to prep for college. She said most of us weren't college material. I chuckle now because two of the boys she threw out of her office got doctorate degrees despite her condescension. Her favorite line was "you'll never make it to college." Looking back, I could have been a better student, especially in history and math.

After high school, I linked history with art and that is when I began to love history, through art.

Our English teacher, Mr. K, took us to Broadway shows often, introduced us to live theater. The musicals were popular in the sixties, and Broadway was a family destination to see current shows. Mr. K is still remembered whenever old classmates talk about the theater.

After high school, I would NOT go to college. I had little interest in becoming a teacher, a nurse, or a housewife too soon. In the sixties, women didn't have too many choices, but soon there would be feminists, like Gloria Steinman, who led the charge for women to choose beyond becoming housewives. I jumped onboard. Boys thought being a feminist meant women hated men. I rebelled at six years old, especially after being taunted in my snowsuit leggings.

Many classmates went straight into college, and most of the girls went to secretarial school, which landed them a good salary before getting married. The boys usually got their first summer jobs on Wall Street. Many remained working the stock market. Boys were expected to be men after high school. They were the breadwinners. This meant learning a new skill or going to a four-year college.

Some boys and girls fell in love in high school. When they held hands walking down the halls, this meant they were a couple. Most of us were more inclined to talk about someone we liked for hours on the telephone.

We had one wall phone and an extension phone upstairs with long curly wires. Siblings fought hard for a turn to make their phone calls. Try and talk a teenager out of getting off a long call that was "very important."

Telephone booths were placed strategically throughout America. The island maintained a row of booths inside the ferry terminal, and there were booths at bus stop corners. Phones were at many corners and if running late, a phone call was expected. We carried loose change.

My friends, who took the bus home after school, were photographed by a journalist from the local newspaper, the *Staten Island Advance*. He happened to see the girls huddled inside the phone booth during a torrential downpour. They were on Castleton Corners here and ran for cover in the phone booth.

Photo taken of Curtis friends Audrey, Mary and Suzanne, in 1960 as a news photographer passed by.

It was easy to be influenced by the poets. We studied Emily Dickenson, Robert Frost, Rudyard Kipling, Edna St. Vincent Millay, Carl Sandburg, Henry Wadsworth Longfellow, Edgar Allen Poe, Walt Whitman, Tennessee Williams, and of course all of Shakespeare's books and poems. In class, we had long discussions covering these prominent poets.

We read Ayn Rand's thick books, *The Fountainhead* and *Atlas Shrugged*. We also read *Tom's Cabin, Catcher in the Rye,* which had not been banned in New York, *War and Peace*, and *The Carpetbaggers*. We loved the southern romance *Gone with the Wind*. Classics and biographies from Abe Lincoln and Anne Frank to George Carver Washington and American Indian chiefs, like Geronimo and Black Elk. We learned about their battles and the real native Americans, not cowboys versus Indians.

Having access to the library

when it was closed on Sunday helped me get my last-minute homework done. I included any friends who missed the library for an upcoming assignment. We were often so busy with our sports that we waited until the last minute, which is when living in the library came in handy.

I found out that becoming a cheerleader was a journey and a challenge. There was hard work and winning that we strived for—to be the best of all teams within New York City. There were, of course, wins and losses. It was probably one of the best experiences of my lifetime in preparation for the real world where setting goals and organization were necessary to compete.

It was easy to be popular and liked by most of the boys. But that also meant that many would never ask a cheerleader for a date. I dated the captain, Tony L. Cheerleaders dated football and basketball players. We had over 500 students in my graduating class alone.

Joining social clubs was important at Curtis. These clubs offered a creative outlet. For those who wanted to excel in a subject, a club was joined. I would have belonged to a writing or theater club, but cheerleading took up all my free time.

On my way to an away football game, Staten Island Ferry

Sigrid and I practiced together for the auditions. We went downstairs to the library children's room on weekends and moved the tables and chairs out of the way to practice cartwheels and high jumps into the air. We practiced at the park, even the beach, to perfect each of the cheers required to be considered for this elite group. Arms and hands had to be perfectly executed in sync with our cheers.

Competing with 250 girls from freshman to juniors made it almost impossible. Let's say it was a longshot. It occurred to me that no "who you knew" or "favors" were granted. Choices were made mainly on ability and, yes, looks and personality. Every year replacements for the graduating cheerleaders were needed. Miss M, our coach, granted the final approval based on personality and grades.

There were only five openings. From P.S. 16, Sigrid and I made the cut. Eventually Eileen made the team the next year, with a little help in practice from me. Marian made the Majorettes squad as did her sister, Anita, the following year. My new friends, from other elementary schools in the area joined one of the two squads. Suzanne made cheerleaders. Audrey, Diana, Dee, and Syd became Majorettes. I never thought we would be pals for sixty years, but to this day, we are.

I was a cheerleader for my junior and senior years. We had to keep up with grades. We practiced new jumps and cartwheels to perfect them over summer practice before the football season began. A few of us practiced in the library children's room area. Dad said we were on our own, if anyone got hurt.

We had just enough space to perform in-place cartwheels and jumps with legs very far apart and high in the air. Precision and timing were key. Our goal was to win another first-place championship tournament trophy. Clove Lakes Park was our weekly practice in summer and the Curtis gym or the football field on campus during school term.

I felt a lot more confident as a student being a Curtis High School Warriors cheerleader. I'm sure if we had social media, we would have been bullied because we were popular. It was just perfect the way it was.

Becoming a cheerleader, majorette, or booster for the games had their pluses. We were part of football and basketball season and cheered our fellow team players, boys only, throughout the season. We never gave up screaming out our cheers, regardless of wins or losses. At some

Curtis High Champion Cheerleaders (1961) Weissglass Football Stadium, Staten Island, NY

First place winners of NYC Cheerleading Championship, 1961 (Suzanne, far right, and me, fourth from right)

outdoors games, we were so cold but quickly forgot once we began to cheer our Curtis teams on. "Go Warriors." The squad had already won championship tournaments several years in a row. We wore those gold megaphones, hanging from our long gold chains with a sense of pride for the Curtis High Warriors. After high school, I placed the megaphone in my jewelry box. When I moved to the city, it was stolen along with a white banded watch Uncle Tom, my godfather, bought home from Switzerland where he was stationed with the army during World War II with my other uncles.

The megaphone and the watch, treasures from a young girl's past may be gone, but they're not forgotten.

During football season, we wore football sweaters with white corduroy skirts, slightly above the knees, with maroon panties and thick white socks and saddle shoes. Our basketball uniforms were made to order to fit perfectly. These were the uniforms we wore at the competitions.

Unfortunately, Sigrid's dad bought a home in Port Richmond. She was a trained Curtis cheerleader by then. Her abilities and her Marilyn Monroe look placed her immediately on the Port Richmond High School Squad.

I met Suzanne S at the cheerleading competitive tryouts. It was our sophomore year. Suzanne complained that she was the tallest. But I was typical at five feet three and a half inches.

Curtis Majorettes

One of Suzanne's high school essays, "High Hopes" detailed the competitive practice ordeal. She wrote, "Don't tell anyone about our cheers for the New York City Championship, not even your parents, ordered our Squad Captain. Everything was top secret, as we didn't want to divulge any moves to competing schools. We were determined to do well at this big cheer tournament."

"Despite bruised knees and aching muscles from months of daily practice, we dry-cleaned our burgundy and white corduroy uniforms and polished our brown and white saddle shoes. We bought white leather gloves to make our hand clapping sound louder and sharper. Everywhere we went we'd sing "Heart" from the musical *Damn Yankees*" (courtesy of Suzanne Seeley Beyer, 2006).

Cheerleaders, majorettes, and our Booster Club joined together to sing, "You've Gotta Have Heart" on the bus going to and from away games. Those of us who continued our private reunions, sang again at every one of our get-togethers since the last big class of 1962 reunion in 2002 and our reunion in 2019 at Marian's Florida home.

The cheerleaders attending were Suzanne and me. Audrey was the captain of the majorette squad and Dee was co-captain. The other majorettes were Diana, Marian, and Syd along with Mary, our Cornell graduate who we have met many times since the 2002 reunion. We have coordinated meetings in California, Colorado Springs, Connecticut, Florida, Maine, Maryland, and Texas. The booster club, founded by Mr.

Curtis Booster Club

Vince Speranza, American history teacher, was most valuable. As we found out many years later, on our Curtis '62 Facebook page (organized by Patti Borello), our teacher was an American hero, Airborne soldier at the Battle of the Bulge in World War II. This patriot, at the age of 95, continues to be an inspiration to his kids, us. Liz, who was captain of the boosters keeps in close contact with Mr. Speranza. His book, *Nuts*, details his experiences on the battlefield.

The boosters were an integral part of school spirit and avid fund-raisers too. The Curtis Warriors never failed even when we didn't win a game. We kept our spirit—"Gotta Have Heart."

The years following high school graduation in 1962 were daunting, except for music. President John F. Kennedy was assassinated in 1963. The civil rights marches were front and center. Beatlemania was everywhere. American troops were sent into a combat zone in Vietnam in 1965. Some classmates died on the battlefield while others became ill from contact with Agent Orange, a chemical known to do significant damage. Soldiers from Curtis High Class of '62, Harry Holt and Nick Lia, never made it home. The Vietnam War lasted until 1975.

A Soldier

HENRY WADSWORTH LONGFELLOW

"A soldier of the Union mustered out,"
Is the inscription on an unknown grave
At Newport News, beside the salt-sea wave,
Nameless and dateless; sentinel or scout
Shot down in skirmish, or disastrous rout
Of battle, when the loud artillery drove
Its iron wedges through the ranks of brave
And doomed battalions, storming the redoubt.
Thou unknown hero sleeping by the sea
In thy forgotten grave! with secret shame
I feel my pulses beat, my forehead burn,
When I remember thou hast given for me
All that thou hadst, thy life, thy very name,
And I can give thee nothing in return.

I would learn, through the hardship of a soldier, that the journey into adulthood had its consequences. I moved out of my parents' home thinking that freedom meant I could do anything. I thought I was as free as a bird discovering its wings. So, with every good intention in my heart and a longing to live life to the fullest, I was ready to fly.

CHAPTER SIX

Turning Point
1966–1971

She's Got a Ticket to Ride

—JOHN DENVER

California Dreamin'

The fall of 1966 was a turning point, a portal to adulthood for me.

Helen and Irene taught for the New York City school system. Both sisters had their own apartments in the city.

I completed three years teaching ballroom dance, worked temporary jobs, and studied jazz and tap. I was living at our library apartment, saving money to travel. I remember the day vividly when I moved out of our library apartment, the last of the three library girls to leave the nest. My grammar school friend, Sigrid, came by in her VW bug, bright red, a gift from her parents after college graduation.

We planned to move to San Francisco since it was then a happening place. I'll not forget the look on Mom's face as she looked out the kitchen window, "Call home," Mom said before I left. "Collect call is good too. We want to know you got there safe. If you want to come home, we'll send you a ticket."

Crazy things happened in San Francisco, riots broke out, civil rights were challenged, women wanted equality, and ordinary people were "dropping out" of the doldrums and looking for change.

The next two years I spent in San Francisco's cultural revolution. Psychedelic designs permeated the fabric of the city, as hippies went on "mind blowing" trips. They dressed in tie-dyed loose-fitting scarves and pants and gathered around the parks and streets in record numbers to preach free love and have smoke-ins, mostly weed. We were weekend warriors.

Sigrid and I worked nine to five jobs in order to pay bills and keep a roof over our heads. We rented an apartment overlooking Union Street and the crookedest street in the world, at the corner of Union and Green.

(Above) Me, before leaving for San Francisco

(Right) Standing in front of my apartment on Green St. in San Francisco.

Typing class from high school was the perfect skill the agencies needed for Gal Friday applicants, so I got paid a little more. Our new neighbor had a motorcycle, and he drove me to work almost every day. He cursed at the traffic and flew down the hilly streets of San Francisco, very fast. My neighbor was crazy as a loon, but I liked the adrenaline rush, and I got to my

Grateful Dead concert poster in San Francisco

assigned temporary jobs on time. Sigrid's college degree eventually kicked in for a better paying professional job at Dun and Bradstreet, which eventually sent her Hawaii, where she met her husband.

Putting flowers in my hair and wearing mini-skirts, bell bottoms, and paper dresses didn't make the Hippie Revolution as glamorous as I hoped. But the fashion was young and made a statement that we women were seeking change. At the same time, rock bands' lyrics encouraged experimenting with mind-altering drugs. Many hippies and super rock star bands got hooked on LSD, heroin, cocaine, or weed.

Hippies converged on Haight Ashbury, often living and begging on the street corners. We didn't think the street hippies were "groovy," but the movement of freedom for all remained an appeal as anti-war demonstrators and dropouts crowded the city.

We dated young men who had jobs. We often went to Sausalito and wine country with side trips to Las Vegas and Lake Tahoe, even south to Mexico.

We sang along with the radio's DJs as they played hit songs from the Beach Boys, the Beatles, Carole King, Mammas and Pappas, the Rolling Stones, and the Grateful Dead. The music spoke, and the world listened. Adventure awaited at one's own risk.

The sky was grey and the mood dark with sadness as we witnessed our troops come home from and return to Vietnam over a span of years. They were greeted by war protestors who threw urine and debris at them as they stepped foot onto the very ground they defended. San Francisco was no exception.

One night in 1967 fate would bring me and Sigrid to a downtown pub at the exact same time when two of my our classmates, decided they too would go to that popular night club.

That's where we spotted John M and Tom R across the bar. They were stationed at a base near the Golden Gate Bridge. None of us admitted it, but we were a little homesick for Staten Island and felt a comfort knowing each other.

Sigrid's sister moved in with us in San Francisco. One evening Barbara and I went to a party. Barbara left the party early. Two days later, I had still not come home. Sigrid and Barbara told John and Tom. The concern grew since I hadn't called home. The fabulous four, (Sigrid, Barbara, John and Tom) set out to find me.

John and Tom tracked my steps as best they could as described by Barbara. They never found the house with the white picket fence. Barbara knew only it was in the general vicinity of Haight and Ashbury. My soldier boys were ready to engage in a confrontation with my cute "date." I am glad they didn't find that place. That night was my mistake.

Brownies laced with mind-altering drugs and contents of pills sprinkled on top were on the unwritten menu. I had no idea what I ingested and little recollection of the events following the next four days. These incidents were a common occurrence of the Hippie movement. In San Francisco, we learned that young women were vulnerable to the "free love" hype.

I am not sure if I escaped or just left freely. My exit through the hallways and past the bedrooms, kitchen, and living room revealed a dark place that morning. Stragglers were asleep on couches and the floors. Cigarettes burned in make-shift paper cup ashtrays. The smell of stale beer and the indoor smog of smoke stuck to my nostrils as I passed from the darkness to the daylight. I was no longer a captive of my state of being. I had my phone book and looked up my own phone number to call home. I couldn't remember where I lived but did remember my people. The girls picked me up at the corner of Haight and Ashbury.

It took the next few months to regain some of my memory. San Francisco was about to come to an early good-bye. Eventually, we all parted ways. Sigrid moved to Hawaii, Barbara went back to college, and our soldier boys continued their journeys once their tours of duty ended. California dreaming was all about an era. Leaving flower power to history was never a denial of experiencing the bad with the good. I never regretted any of it, even tripping out. It was a harsh lesson to not trust a stranger I met at a laundromat because he was cute and had a big sweet shaggy dog. Eventually, a year later after returning home, my memory returned.

In early winter of 1968, I boarded a plane back to New York City, glad to see my sisters again who I could tell everything to without Mom and Dad knowing the bad stuff.

Martin Luther King Jr. was assassinated that April. After that, the Civil Rights Act of 1968 was signed by President Johnson. Bobby Kennedy was assassinated following a presidential campaign speech and the United States was gearing up for a landing on the moon set for 1969. At the same time, Vietnam raged on even after my soldier boys returned. I was numb to the horror of war with so many already killed.

I was home and worked temporary jobs in New York as I continued my recuperation. The world was not a perfect place. Mom and Dad never asked about what happened in San Francisco. I never told them, exactly. As soon as I got home, I took out a new library card. I was quieter, more introspective, less giddy. I read more books and researched new places to visit, delaying a return to college. I didn't know the librarians at the St. George Library well because we had our private entrance. Dad liked to introduce his library girls, "This is my baby daughter, Carolyn. She just returned home from California."

The Beatles' *Sergeant Pepper's Lonely-Hearts Club Band* album helped in my recovery. They haven't lost their magic, ever. The Beatles sang in harmony as they spread LOVE throughout the world. John, Paul, and George went to India to study meditation and yoga from Maharishi Mahesh Yogi in 1968. They gave up drugs, and I never ate brownies again. Their next two albums, *White Album* and *Abby Road* were written in India in early 1968.

Joined by the Internet in 2002, my soldier boys and I attended our 40th Curtis High School reunion, all three of us, holding hands, the old scars less of a burden. We were the same yet our experiences so different. The time we spent in San Francisco lived another day. We were a team once, young and hopeful. We rehashed all that stuff and how comforting it was they had their Staten Island girls around for a while. And, I was thrilled to have them back home again.

Holding hands was the perfect medicine this time around.

Europe

It was time for my next adventure to begin in the summer of 1968. Eric Fromm's *Europe on $5 a Day* was every traveler's bible. The Eurail pass was about $75 in 1968. We went first class on a budget. One could travel to any country on one Eurail Pass with an American passport.

That summer I flew on Sabena Airlines to Belgium and took my first trip on the Eurail to Germany where I made a connection to Hamburg. It felt a bit like time travelling. The ambiance was reminiscent of a war-torn city, even though Germany had rebuilt slowly over the years post World War II with America's help. Once Hitler and the Nazis were gone, they left behind a footprint of darkness. I felt it that first day the train pulled into the station.

On the train, the conductor was tucked into a stiff uniform. He may have been a soldier. In German, the soldier put his hand out near my face and spoke his native language, "Reispass bitte, Reispass bitte."

I knew it sounded a lot like passport and others in my compartment took out their passports, so I followed along. The conductor stamped it Hamburg, Germany. As the train pulled into the station, I could see German written everywhere and on billboards around the station. Of course, I was in Germany, not New York's German Town, I told myself. Europe was so different from the United States. It was the old country where so many immigrants left for America, including my own grandparents who came in from Italy and Poland. Our families never said much about their roots. They were American now and didn't look back.

Outside the train station's American Express Office Mail Depot, I met a German gentleman who pointed me in the direction of the address Barbara wrote on her postcard, which was waiting for me at the Hamburg American Express office.

Barbara was staying with relatives. She was born in Germany. It was all so comforting for me to know I was with someone who would take me to interesting places not tourist destinations. I would have been lost in Hamburg and did not speak the language. I got the insider tour from Barbara who spoke fluent German and stayed at the family house where only German was spoken.

The next day, I drove with Barbara and her cousin to the Rhine River, past its historic castles and into the quaint towns where a heavy stein of beer was in the hand of most Germans, lunch or dinner. I was filled with a new excitement since my parents never took us to Europe. Germany's Rhineland, surrounded by mountains, has its beer gardens tucked away, wineries, pretty flowers, and smiling faces. I liked their stories of olden days and cobblestone streets, with winding pathways. Many of the German college boys we met in our travels spoke English. Inside the beer gardens, they held their hands tightly around their beer steins as they toasted each other and us, the American girls. We welcomed each other's cultures with open ears and hearts.

After leaving Germany, I arrived in Paris. Sister Helen and her successful Parisian artist boyfriend waited for me to ring their bell. They lived in a loft overlooking the River Seine. Mom and Dad didn't know they lived together. They would not have approved. Helen and Jean Christian lived on St. Germain-des-Pres. That was a romantic relationship that lasted many years.

Helen was extraordinary and Jean was a well-educated, charming Frenchman. Paris held a mystique unlike any other city with its architecture, churches, cafes, and museums. Helen had only two days with me. She was on her way to Greece for a week.

American Express Offices were in every European city for mail delivery and pick up. It was our main communication while we were traveling. I never missed a letter from home or a postcard. Audrey got mail from her boyfriend in most places. Below are some of those postcards I saved over the years. They were tucked in between other photos. I suppose they were meant for a higher purpose, this memoir, and to learn that present day postcards could not replicate the photographic scenes from those days.

Helen and Jean in Paris

The post cards home:

June 26, 1968

Arrived in Brussels, mailing from Hamburg. I'm onboard the train now heading for Hamburg. Exciting things and people. Outside of language barrier, and time change I'm getting along. What an education. It's going to be a good two months. Take care.

July 3

The picture card is one of the seven wonders of the world. The Mannequin 'Pis'. Can't imagine why! (ha) Leaving out of Brussels, Barb, Mary and I drove in Barbara's new VW, bought in Germany. We stayed with Mary's relatives. Most gracious people. day we spent the day in Fecamp, northern coastal area. We leave after breakfast for Paris. Will be here July 3-July 10. Meet Audrey July 7. Write to Madrid or Lisbon. We'll eventually get there. Enjoy your summer bungalow.

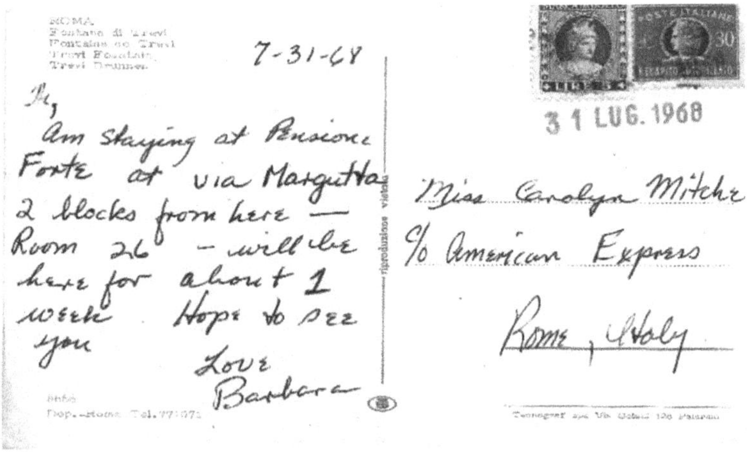

ROMA
Fontana di Trevi

7-31-68

Hi,
Am staying at Pensione Forte at via Margutta 2 blocks from here — Room 26 — will be here for about 1 week. Hope to see you
Love
Barbara

31 LUG. 1968

Miss Carolyn Mitche
c/o American Express
Rome, Italy

Postcards sent home from Europe. Top postcard, under a bridge on the Seine, Paris.

July 8

Still in Paris, Met up with Audrey. We leave for Bordeaux the 11th to 14th. Then Lisbon from 16th to 17th. Then Majorca and Madrid from the 20th July. Helen left Paris yesterday and travelling. All is calm in Paris. Sorbonne no new riots. Parisians drink café all day and walk along the Seine. If emergency, Blue Cross/Blue Shield has emergency locators. Love to Irene.

August 5

Got your letter in Rome. On train heading for Florence. Love Italy. Will meet up again with Barbara after August 10, when my Eurail pass runs out. Continue travel by car to Venice. Audrey and I will go to Austria, Innsbruck and Zurich. I was excited to hear you took off for Chicago. Missed Helen in Rome

August 19

Happy Birthday Mom! Leaving Vienna on 14th as I told you. Will split from all and go to London where I meet a San Francisco friend who lives in London. In Frankfort, Germany, August 22nd and meet Helen the 30th is the plan.

August 21, 1968

Stopped here in Heidelberg to visit castles. Leave for Frankfort. Audrey will drive with Barbara and I will fly to London, student fare.

Irene traveled back and forth to London and Wales on sabbaticals and summer vacation from teaching in Harlem. The summer I was in Europe, Irene was in Mexico. Irene was writing books of poetry. She began to publish in literary journals. Irene spoke fluent Spanish and soon taught Vietnamese children English after the Vietnam War.

Audrey and I also visited the Austrian Alps. That was quite a day. Eventually, we had lunch and beer with some Austrian college students and since the air was

Irene in Wales

My adventures in the Austrian Alps

so thin, so high up, we both needed help getting back down. Yes, the beer got to us very quickly.

There were a few stories I didn't write home about. There were the two handsome journalists Audrey and I met in Roma and me on water skis in Majorca hanging on for dear life at 60 miles per hour barreling toward the shoreline. And, then there was the time I almost choked to death in a restaurant over Chateaubriand. Audrey and a waiter performed the Heimlich maneuver, which probably saved me. I was robbed once in an Austrian hostel.

It was the first and last time Audrey and I stayed in one. I had hand-picked gifts for friends and family, and in the morning, they were all gone.

I stayed with a friend from San Francisco in London. It only lasted one night after her boyfriend moved in. After Audrey left, I rented a nice flat with breakfast in London. I saw the best of theater London

Me, modeling my new fashions from Europe, St. George Library

had to offer. Sammy Davis Jr. was in town. I wasn't so lonely going to the theater and to my favorite Chinese restaurant. I met a psychic at a theater performance. He predicted I would live a long time and have a son, which was true.

There was a lot to digest on the flight home to Kennedy Airport. The night before I packed all the beautiful soft leather shoes I bought in Venice, Italy. London had a top reputation in fashion. I bought suits and winter tops. The European trip was a course in history, but I loved getting back to my attic room with the cubby nook at St. George Library apartment.

Mom and I at the summer place, Huguenot, Staten Island, torn down to make way for a shoreline parkway.

After Europe, I took dance classes in the city and worked part time. I moved into an apartment with roommates on West 56th Street. I bought my first convertible, a Dodge Dart. It was beautiful but not reliable. Dad liked to tinker with it.

By 1971 I was accepted into the first theater arts program at College of Staten Island (then Richmond College). This was the upper two year program for a bachelor degree. I directed and choreographed a Renaissance and Medieval Dance Troupe. We performed at Lincoln Center. I found my place.

CHAPTER SEVEN

Curtain Call
1971–1976

All the world's a stage, All the men and women merely players
—SHAKESPEARE

MY STATEN ISLAND APARTMENT was within walking distance to classes. I could look out at the World Trade Center Twin Towers in the background, a view I never thought could ever change in my lifetime. We must never forget.

Richard Nixon was president, Carol King's album *Tapestry* was in every home. The United States had already been to the Moon and back in 1969. By 1971, Apollo 14 was the third mission to land on the moon. I had my feet on the ground once I was accepted into the theater arts program at Richmond College on Staten Island (now, College of Staten Island). After Europe and living in the city with roommates coming and going, I was ready to get a degree. My parents had hoped it would be in teaching, like my two brilliant sisters.

There was a building at the corner of Hyatt Street in St. George, where a small round theater was situated to accommodate our productions. The great thing is that after I sold the Dodge Dart, I didn't need a car to get to classes. Everything was within walking distance of the library and my apartment on St. Marks Place.

Rooftop of my new apartment in 1971, St. Marks Place with the Twin Towers in background—A view that one day would change, unexpectedly. The world as I once knew it would never be the same, my New York City.

Review by Richard Kornberg, "The Bald Soprano"

... evening of theatre.

Nothing however can be faulted with th John Hancock dominated production ("The Bald Soprano." The work, directe with the assistance of Marty Sokoloff, is a essay of style, wit and beauty.

We are presented two pairs of Britis couples whose boredom reaches the height of their upper-middleclassness. An intimat gathering is on the evening's agenda and al the action revolves around this event, o non-event.

"The Bald Soprano's" accent is intensel verbal, a mixture of nonsequiturs, which i delivered correctly, result in a totally cohesive, supremely funny playlet. This is precisely what the audiences at 350 St. Marks Place encountered at this excellant Richmond College production.

The tightly knit, smooth as silk direction elicited ensemble acting at its best. However, even in a group effort there are always one or two performers who stand out. In this case Yvonne Fisher and Carolyn Mitchell took the laurels. This in no way diminishes the very real talents of Jack Negri, Tony Cipolla, Dan Crotty and Tony Mullen, the four males who complete the cast.

The varied voacl inflections of Miss Fisher and Miss Mitchell add immeasurably to the evening's enjoyment. While their styles differed—Yvonne Fisher favoring the extended twisting of sylables altering a meaning in midstream as compared with Carolyn Mitchell's perfectly timed blaseness—the ultimate result was a high brand of humor.

The director of the first theater arts program, John Hancock, was known at the time for his movie *Bang the Drum Slowly,* Robert DeNiro's first acting film. Mr. H knew how to get the best out of us in production. As a result, we had many fine plays produced with our small class of actors. Attending our productions were some well-known actors who gave us feedback. New York City is the perfect place to study acting.

I kept one review from my second production, "The Bald Soprano," a play written by Ionesco. Stage fright creeped in the first night that Hector Elonzado, a famous actor, was in the audience. I kept up with the dance classes in the city and attended the American Academy of Dance and Theatre in the West Village. That's where I worked on choreography and performed in musical theatre. I didn't know it at the time, that summer at the academy, but I learned confidence to become a director the following semester.

I saturated myself into New York City's culture. Mayor John Lindsay introduced a policy early in his term as New York City's mayor. He created an office for film and television production. It brought money into the city and brought local jobs known as "supernumeraries" for actors in television and films as well. It was a quick $50 a day and lunch. My soon to be husband, Julian, and I had fun in the crowd filled scenes. He was hired for an entire season at the Lincoln Center Opera. I continued with the dance troupe and worked in off Broadway productions for a while.

We had a small enough group of actors who worked well together. I remember the first time the VCR came into a class, we used it immediately for filming scenes and shorts. It was our "tech tool" of the day. The film crew included the Hamill brothers, Brian and Denis. Brian was a photographer and Denis followed in the footsteps of his brother, Pete Hamill, and became a columnist for the *Daily News* and an author. Actors Ed Hyland and Terry McGiver began work in stage and screen. Ed is now a Broadway actor.

In 1972, my drama professor discussed an opportunity he had in mind for me. Dr. Victor Mattfield was a professor as well as the director of the Classical Music Society. The Music Department had acquired instruments from the Renaissance and Medieval era and needed a choreographer for a special project. I was flabbergasted that he asked me! Was I good enough to take this project on? Mr. Hancock, a Hollywood movie director and my advisor, said I certainly could do it. He would give me credits toward my degree if I accepted the assignment.

There's one thing that never failed me—my imagination.

Professor Mattfeld was a scholar and easy to work with. I knew nothing about the instruments from the Renaissance and Medieval era but would learn from his musicians. They played sackbuts, zinks, krumhorns, lutes, cornenuses, rebecs, organettos, and bells. The music was soothing. I closed my eyes as the music wrote the scenes for me. I wrote the screenplay within a setting of a 13th- to 14th-century royal ballroom.

I found out there was little information on the dances dating to this time. However, the librarian at the fairly new library at Lincoln Center went the extra distance and had some books waiting for me on my next visit. Since she had met my dad, she knew I was a library girl and we formed a special bond.

The books by Thoinot Arbeau, Pierre Ataignant, and Claude Gervaiseon had information about folk-type dances and were written in French. I had a lot to work to do. My high school French came in handy for interpretations. I knew I had to add a lot more pizzazz to these steps. I summoned my sister Helen, who danced with the Mary Anthony Dance Company. She got some dancers to sign on. I got a few dancers from my theater group and one from the Academy of Arts and Music, which I attended over the summer. All I could offer the dancers was a reference, no pay.

The next step was to bring the dance, music and song together. My fiancé, Julian, although reluctant to wear knickers, joined the troupe when a male dancer left. Julian planned the songs to add to the dance and music. We got a soprano and a tenor from the music director. Next, came the costumes, which was coordinated from the music department. Julian and I went to the city

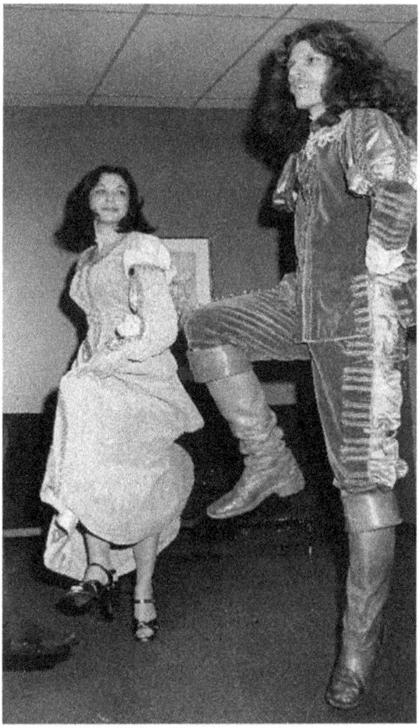

Me and Marty Albucher performing a demonstration for the newspapers.

to pick up all the costumes at a theater production rental company. It was a miracle in the making. Once we put on those gowns and the men wore their fancy regalia, we were ready for the first performance in November 1973 at the Richmond College Lecture Hall. It was a success.

After that, I applied for a grant from the Council of the Arts on Staten Island. Funding came and we performed at parks on Staten Island and then to the Cloisters and all around the state of New York at various events.

A year later, Con Edison sponsored a community holiday festival at Lincoln Center for the performing arts and my troupe was asked to perform. "A Staten Island Holiday" also included other companies. It was a night to remember. The notes on the Lincoln Center program wrote about my troupe's origin. The program stated, "Since then the Troupe has worked independently presenting various programs around the City and working on filming. This rather unique dance company may be only one of three such companies in the country. Tonight they perform the dances and music of an actual 14th Century Ballroom."

(Back row, center to right) Helen, Marty, me and Julian at the Lincoln Center.

Dance Troupe at Lincoln Center, the Paven and The Galliarde

THE LIBRARY GIRLS

Library Girl #1 | Helen Mitchell, Textile Artist

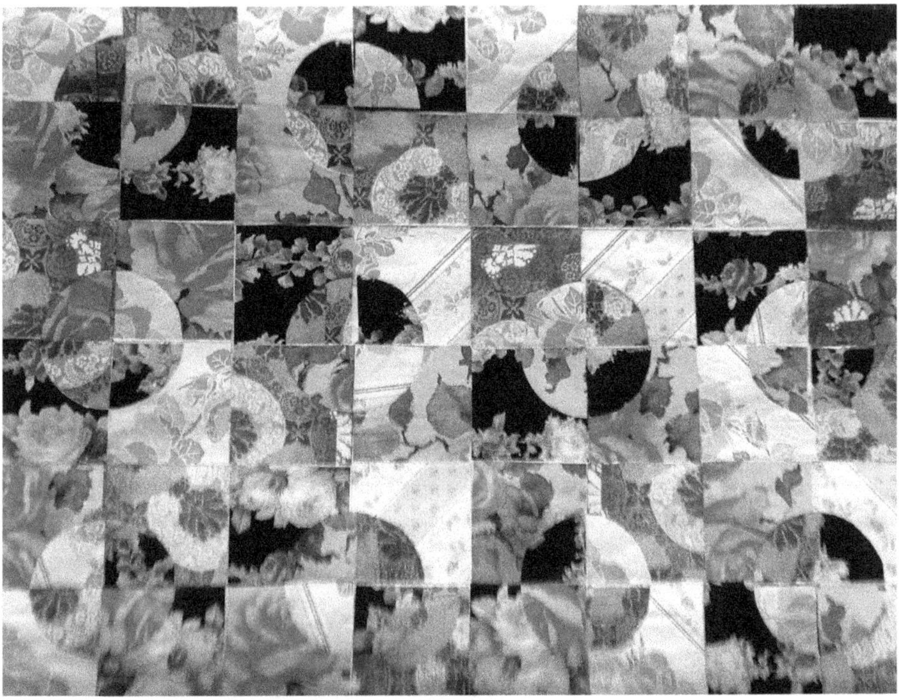

Geometric Kaleidoscope, multimedia by Helen Mitchell

Iris Suite, courtesy of Helen Mitchell, paint, paper, beads

Library Girl #2 | Irene Mitchell, Lyric Poet

Much Obliged

I'd been thinking scarlet
when I saw him,
a tanager,
just him, not her,
on a limb and calling.

I don't mean to imply
that scarlet is exceedingly precious
for a bridegroom in a bower.
However, our meeting was rare.

I dared to greet him in my way.
You cannot know how imperceptibly
I craved
some discordant reality.

Celebrating light,
as when one flies from the mainland
to the luxuriant,
we sang a song as dulcet
as a rooster's *[illegible]*.

He was my tanager, so primo in array,
and I was his scarlet sonata.

"Much Obliged," courtesy of Irene Mitchell from A Study of Extremes in Six Suites *(Cherry Grove Collections).*

Irene Mitchell reads in Woodstock, New York, from her collection Minding the Spectrum's Business *(FutureCycle Press).*

Library Girl #3 | Carolyn Mitchell Rhodes, Author

Me and son, Casey Julian on ferry

This memoir covers the years from the 1930s to the mid-1970s, the years leading up to and growing up inside the library when Dad worked there.

When he retired from NYPL in 1975, Theresa and Joseph moved to Toms River, New Jersey. Dad continued to play ball with a senior team and won the Babe Ruth Award from the New Jersey governor. Mom and Dad passed away, well into their 80s at their home in Toms River.

I became a mother to Casey Julian. John Julian Rhodes, a lyricist, guitarist, songwriter, and singer, unexpectedly passed away in 1990 at the age of forty. Our son is an electronics technology expert.

Helen and Irene retired from teaching. They both honed their talents past retirement. They continue to travel and stay active as creative and professional artists.

The Commemorative Bronze was never left behind because Dad wrote "KEEP THIS" on the description of the Bronze. At the time of his death in the 1990s, I took it with me and placed it a closet. Occasionally, I would admire it. I lost it and found it again during my many moves.

Patience and Fortitude, the two proud lion mascots who guard the NYPL main branch entrance, may have had something to do with inspiring me to never lose it or forget it. I kept the bronze medal commemorating the NYPL 50th anniversary in 1961.

For the NYPL's 75th anniversary of the Central Research Library in 1986, all staff members from the 85 libraries received *The New York Public Library, Its Architecture and Decoration,"* by Henry Hope Reed. Such dedication from NYPL philanthropists. The early pioneers should never be forgotten. Brooke Astor, Andrew Heiskell, Vartan Gregorian, and Mr. Reed, the author, have spent many years making the book possible and giving us a free library system. They signed each book to all staff members in the five boroughs of New York City.

Every year, I read through it again. I am a library kid who admires the architectural details of the special book. Every statue, especially the one, "Lady of the Bath," Dad kept clean in his first job at NYPL is a favorite remembrance. Every statue inside and out, I study with a new set of eyes. Dad always said knowledge is power.

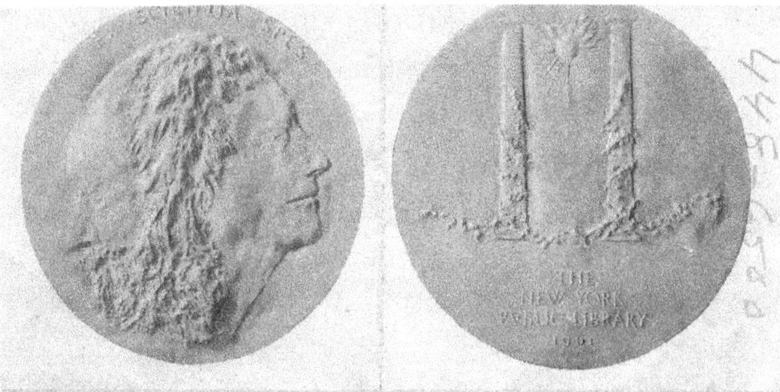

THE NEW YORK PUBLIC LIBRARY MEDAL
COMMEMORATING THE 50TH ANNIVERSARY OF THE LIBRARY AT FIFTH AVENUE AND 42ND STREET

May 23, 1961

KEEP THIS

On May 23, 1911, President William Howard Taft dedicated The New York Public Library building at Fifth Avenue and 42nd Street "to the spread of knowledge among the people." On the same date in 1961, on the occasion of its 50th anniversary, the Library's Trustees rededicated the building, its vast research collections and its staff to the furtherance of public knowledge and enlightenment in the years ahead. In honor of the 50th anniversary this medal was executed. Its design is the work of Leonard Baskin, noted young American artist and sculptor.

Four of these bronze, torch-finished medals were struck for presentation to those institutions and individuals who have contributed significantly to the advancement of research libraries, and a limited number of medals were struck in smaller size to be given to guests attending the Library's 50th anniversary celebration.

THE DESIGN

The medal's obverse expresses the theme EX SCIENTIA SPES ("from knowledge, hope"). The elderly sage looking downward represents the learning and wisdom of the past; the upward-looking youth reflects hope through his aspiration to knowledge. This concept has its origin in a private book plate suggested by Julius S. Held, Professor of Fine Arts at Barnard College, Columbia University, and executed by Mr. Baskin.

The reverse of the medal symbolizes the New York Public Library as a "gateway to light and learning" by the use of two classical columns through which are seen the rays of light or pure learning, and rays of heat or applied learning. The garlands reflect the fruits of knowledge and suggest further the rewards associated with books and libraries.

THE ARTIST

Leonard Baskin is Associate Professor of Art at Smith College, Northampton, Massachusetts, where he has taught sculpture, drawing and printmaking since 1953. Born in New Brunswick, New Jersey, on August 15, 1922, Baskin studied in Paris with the sculptor, Maurice Glickman, from 1937 to 1939. Subsequently, he attended the School of Architecture and Allied Arts of New York University (1939 to 1941) and the School of Fine Arts at Yale University (1940 to 1943). After the war he continued his studies at the New School for Social Research in New York City and received the Bachelor of Arts degree in 1949.

Baskin has been awarded numerous prizes and fellowships including: the Louis Comfort Tiffany Foundation Fellowship for Sculpture in 1947; Guggenheim Fellowship in Creative Printmaking in 1953; and the 1961 Grant in Graphics from the National Institute of Arts and Letters.

His works are included in the collections of the Metropolitan Museum of Art, the Museum of Modern Art, Whitney Museum of Art, Brooklyn Museum, The National Gallery of Art and The Library of Congress in Washington, D. C., Fogg Museum of Art, Museum of Fine Arts in Boston, Worcester Museum of Art, Seattle Art Museum, Philadelphia Museum of Art, and City Art Museum of St. Louis.

THE NEW YORK PUBLIC LIBRARY

The New York Public Library at Fifth Avenue and 42nd Street, in addition to being the administrative center of the Public Library System's 80 branches, houses reference collections which contain close to fifty centuries of human thought and experience, recorded in every known language and dialect. These collections grew out of the consolidation in 1895 of the Astor and Lenox private libraries with the Tilden Trust. Today, among the Library's 13 million items are many treasures of civilized man including the first Gutenberg Bible to come to this country; the Bay Psalm Book; quarto and folio editions of Shakespeare; the Lenox Globe of 1510—the first globe to depict the New World; Jefferson's handwritten draft of the Declaration of Independence; and Washington's manuscript of his Farewell Address.

The Fifth Avenue Library is supported largely by private endowments and annual gifts from private sources. The commissioning of the 50th Anniversary Medal was made possible through the generosity of a friend of the Library.

Circa 1996, I rented a Victorian home in the town of Eutaw, Alabama, only a half-hour drive to the University of Alabama where I worked. Later, I moved to Tuscaloosa, Alabama, after Casey Julian graduated from Warrior Academy. I call it home now—well, it's my home away from home sweet home.

The Library Girls in Eutaw, Alabama

CAROLYN RHODES has been recognized for her published articles, essays and blogs, and has won several writing awards. She lives in Tuscaloosa, Alabama, her home for the past twenty-five years. Carolyn's New York City roots are evident to all who meet her. In her memoir, ***Library Girls of New York,*** she shares her experiences while growing up inside two New York Public Carnegie live-in libraries (NYPL). It is a unique and true story which covers the years from 1930s until her Dad retired from the NYPL, mid-1970s. Carolyn retired from the University of Alabama (worked in Birmingham and Tuscaloosa) where she wrote feature articles and edited publications. Presently, she is an exercise instructor for Osher Lifelong Learning Institute (OLLI) located on the campus of the University of Alabama in Tuscaloosa. When Carolyn is not writing, she is line dancing several days a week.

CPSIA information can be obtained
at www.ICGtesting.com
Printed in the USA
JSHW011116261119
2643JS00005B/27

9 781733 916554